ON HISTORY

ON HISTORY

Oliver Stone
and
Tariq Ali
in Conversation

Haymarket Books
Chicago, Illinois

First published in 2011 by
Haymarket Books
P.O. Box 180165
Chicago, IL 60618
773-583-7884
info@haymarketbooks.org
www.haymarketbooks.org

Trade distribution:
In the US, Consortium Book Sales and Distribution, www.cbsd.com
In the UK, Turnaround Publisher Services, www.turnaround-uk.com
In Canada, Publishers Group Canada, www.pgcbooks.ca
In Australia, Palgrave Macmillan, www.palgravemacmillan.com.au
All other countries, Publishers Group Worldwide, www.pgw.com

ISBN: 978-1-60846-149-3

Cover design by Amy Balkin.

This book was published with the generous support of Lannan Foundation and
the Wallace Global Fund.

Printed in the United States.

Library of Congress Cataloging in Publication data is available.

10 9 8 7 6 5 4 3 2 1

Contents

Preface

In early 2009, I received a phone call from Paraguay. It was Oliver Stone. He had been reading *Pirates of the Caribbean: Axis of Hope*, my collection of essays on the changing politics of Latin America, and asked if I was familiar with his work. I was, especially the political films in which he challenged the fraudulent accounts of the war in Vietnam that had gained currency during the B-movie years of Reagan's presidency.

Stone had actually fought in that war in the US Infantry, which made it difficult for others to pigeonhole him as a namby-pamby pacifist. Many of his detractors had avoided the draft and were now making up for it by proclaiming that the war could have been won, had the politicians not betrayed the generals. This enraged Stone, who detested the simplistic recipes now on offer in every aspect of American domestic and external politics. In the original *Wall Street* (1987), for instance, he had depicted the close links between crime and financialized capitalism that ultimately led to the crash of 2007.

The war in Vietnam played a large part in shaping Stone's radical take on his own country. One of the film *JFK*'s most striking scenes, almost ten minutes in length, portrays a talking-heads duo: Jim Garrison (Kevin Costner) and an unidentified military intelligence officer (Donald Sutherland) as they are walking by the Potomac River in Washington, DC, discussing who killed Kennedy. The Sutherland character links the president's execution to his decision to withdraw US troops from Vietnam some months previously. For me, it is—together with the depiction of French officers calmly justifying torture in Gillo Pontecorvo's classic *Battle of Algiers* and the Greek far-right plotting to kill the leftwing deputy Lambrakis in Costa-Gavras's *Z*—one of the three finest scenes in political cinema.

A steady flow of jeremiads from critics on the left and the right denounced this particular scene in Stone's *JFK* as pure fantasy. Later research, however, including the recently published biography of one of the Kennedy administration's leading hawks, McGeorge Bundy, has overwhelmingly vindicated his approach. Kennedy had indeed decided to pull out, largely on the advice of retired General Douglas MacArthur, who told him the war could never be won.

Stone's refusal to accept establishment "truths" is the most important aspect of his filmography. He may get it wrong, but he always challenges imperial assumptions. That is why he traveled to Paraguay to talk to the new president there—a defrocked bishop, weaned on liberation theology, who had succeeded in electorally toppling the long dictatorship of a single party. Fernando Lugo had become part of the new Bolivarian landscape, one that included Hugo Chávez in Venezuela, Evo Morales in Bolivia, and Rafael Correa in Ecuador, flanked by the Kirchners in Argentina, and defended, until his departure, by Lula in Brazil.

Stone asked whether we could meet to discuss his most ambitious project, a twelve-hour documentary series entitled *The Untold History of the United States*. A month later, we met up in Los Angeles. He explained why he felt this project was so necessary. There was a shocking lack of information in the country about its own past, he said, let alone the rest of the world. The receding memory of US citizens was not an accident. "For decades now the kids are either being taught rubbish prepackaged as history modules or nothing," he told me. He regarded this television history as being, in some ways, his most important work. It would present a historical narrative of the United States and how it be came an empire. He interviewed me on film for seven hours, with a few breaks for water (both drinking and passing). Some of my books were by his side, heavily underlined. It was a stimulating experience, devoid of melancholy or sentimentality on either side. He had a job to do, and got on with it. The result, with some cosmetic editing, is the book you have before you.

Until then, I had assumed that Stone's recent tour of South America was for *The Untold History*, but this turned out not to be the case. Angered by the crude assaults on the new leaders by US television networks, as well as the print media (the *New York Times* was a serial offender), Stone had decided to offer the much traduced elected politicians a voice. But he and his producers,

Robert Wilson and Fernando Sulichin, now felt the film had become too bogged down on US media terrain. They asked me to view a rough cut. It was a well-meaning but confusing effort. It simply did not work. Given the scorn Stone's enemies were likely to heap on the film, regardless of its quality, it was best to reduce the number of hostages. Could it be rescued, Wilson wanted to know. I suggested that the existing structure be discarded. I also suggested the valuable archive and a few interviews that should be retained and reinserted in a new version.

In the new commentary that they asked me to write, I concentrated on the strengths of the footage Stone had amassed on his whirlwind two-week tour. This film, in sharp contradistinction to the mesmeric *Comandante*, Stone's seventy-five-minute filmed interview with Fidel Castro, released in 2003, could be much more playful. The resulting documentary was *South of the Border*. The initial research and script were constructed by cowriter Mark Weisbrot and was reedited as a political road movie with a straightforward narrative. A radical and legendary Hollywood filmmaker, angered by what he is watching on his television screen, decides to hop on a plane. In moving and simple terms, the documentary states the case for the changes taking place in South America.

It does not set out to be an analytical, distanced, cold-blooded view of leaders desperate to free themselves from the stranglehold of the Big Brother up north. The film is sympathetic to their cause, which is essentially a cry for freedom, the interviews with the seven elected presidents forming its spinal cord. Chávez is given center stage because he was the pioneering leader of the radical social-democratic experiments currently under way in the continent, and his country has large oil reserves. "If the film convinces people that Chávez is a democratically elected president and not the evil dictator depicted in much of the Western media," Stone said, "we will have achieved our purpose."

It's a tall order these days, but nonetheless was worth a try. A typical gringo criticism of the documentary was that, in his voice-over, Stone can't even pronounce Chávez's name (he says *Shah*-vez, not *Chah*-vess). Interesting that this barely ruffles a feather in Latin America. A mispronunciation of a name is the least of their problems. I have yet to meet a gringo (friend or enemy) who can pronounce my name properly, but it's not a reason to regard a person as intellectually impoverished.

There is another view of the film that we encountered from some Latin American academics working in the United States: that it is too simple. Here we plead guilty. It was never intended to be a tract or a debate. Stone knows his country and its citizens and their viewing habits: *South of the Border* was designed to raise a few questions in their minds. Not that Europe is a great deal better. The hostility to the Bolivarian leaders is pretty universal in the European media, as well, with a few partial exceptions. Strange that a world that bleats on endlessly about democracy has become so hostile to any attempts at economic and political diversity.

Venezuela's late great novelist Rómulo Gallegos wrote in 1935 of Venezuelan history as "a fierce bull, its eyes covered and ringed through the nose, led to the slaughterhouse by a cunning little donkey." No longer. What impressed Stone was that the cunning oligarchs of the two-party system had been defeated and that the bull was free. *The Untold History of the United States*—currently scheduled to be aired in late 2011 or early 2012 by Showtime—will explain at length why the donkeys were given power in the first place.

More than three thousand people, mostly poor and indigenous, attended the film's premiere in Cochabamba, Bolivia, and cheered their side without restraint. "They knew instinctively who the baddies were," Stone told me in New York. "Unlike here." The *New York Times* assigned a veteran hack from the Reagan era—a staunch supporter of the Contras in Nicaragua—to interview us. Perhaps it was tit-for-tat: they wanted to punish us for the disobliging references to the "paper of record" in the documentary. At times it felt as if we were being questioned by a Cold War spook after a trip to a forbidden country. The result was a predictable hack job.

What next? Over dinner at Stone's house, with his Korean partner Sun-jung, their intelligent fourteen-year-old daughter (the real inspiration for *The Untold History*), and his feisty eighty-seven-year-old French mother, Jacqueline Goddet, the director asked jokingly whether there were any strong characters left to consider for a movie. "Lenin or Robespierre?" I inquired hopefully. He turned to his mother, a staunch and devout Gaullist, who couldn't believe her ears. "Robespierre?" she repeated. "Assassin!" That in itself would never be sufficient reason for Oliver not to embark on such a project. An old sinner can't be stopped from casting the penultimate stone.

—Tariq Ali

Chapter 1

From the Russian Revolution to the Second World War

Oliver Stone: I've always wanted to meet you, and I'm glad to have you here in Los Angeles, and to share this time together. It's really an honor, thank you.

Tariq Ali: My pleasure.

I'd like to get right into it and ask you about a strong thesis in your book *Pirates of the Caribbean*, regarding the Russian Revolution. What was its impact on America and what was its impact on the world?

Let us just start with the First World War, which probably was the single most important event of the twentieth century, not recognized as such. We mainly think about the Second World

War and Hitler, but it was the First World War that brought about suddenly the death of a number of empires. The Austro-Hungarian Empire collapsed. The Ottoman Empire collapsed. The tsarist empire in Russia collapsed. And on the heels of this arose nationalism, communism, revolutionary movements of different kinds. The Russian Revolution probably would not have happened in that particular way had there not been a First World War, which broke up the old ruling classes, brought an end to the old order. In February 1917, the war is going badly. Russia is in revolution, the tsar has been overthrown. And in February 1917, coincidentally, the leaders of the United States decide that they're going to enter this war. A total break with isolationism, and feeling that because Europe is changing, and possibly because the changes might threaten them—Bolsheviks are taking over—they have to go in and intervene in this war and sort it out. And suddenly America is aroused. We've got to go and fight the Germans, they want to defeat the Germans. And in goes the United States.

So the First World War is the event that drives the United States away from this part of the world in North America and into Europe, and sets it up on the world stage. And that sets the stage for the big confrontations that we saw in the twentieth century. Because the Russian Revolution had a massive impact. It had not simply toppled the monarchy. After all, that had happened in the French Revolution and in the English one before that. That wasn't new. And the American Revolution had decided to do away with aristocracy and monarchs all together. But it was the hope that came with the Russian Revolution, the feeling that you could change the world for the better, and bring the downtrodden, the wretched of the earth, and put them on a pedestal. That was the aim, that was the hope. And for twenty or thirty years, that hope carried on. It wasn't until much later that people realized that this hadn't worked, that the Russian situation had many, many problems of its own. But just the belief that the working-class movement of the world was going to be elevated had a big impact everywhere, including in the United States. Not just on the rulers, not just on the corporations, but on the labor movement.

I think one should never forget that the United States had a very strong tradition of labor militancy. You had the Wobblies, the Industrial Workers of the World, which united all the migrant workers from all over into one big union. The Wobbly Joe Hill used to take the songs of the Salvation Army, and turn them around: "There'll be pie in the sky when you die." And all these songs brought to life and unified the labor movement in the United States—people from different parts of Europe who didn't even speak the same languages. German, English, Norwegian, Swedish, they became one family.

And there was a lot of repression. People rarely talk about it, but there was a lot of repression carried out by the corporations in the United States against the American working class in the 1920s and the 1930s. And I think that that repression played a big part in preventing the emergence, if you like, of a more socialist, more labor party structure in the United States. Politics got stuck at the top. So the Russian Revolution's impact went very, very deep, and one can't ignore it.

Would you say the United States went into World War I decisively because of the Russian Revolution, or would it have gone anyway? If Russia had withdrawn from the war, Britain and France perhaps would've been overwhelmed by the German military at this point.

Well, I think the combination did it. That the Bolsheviks had raised the demand for land, bread, and peace. They weren't going to fight in this war. And there's no doubt that the Germans would have defeated the French.

There was no doubt?

And the British. There's no doubt that, had the United States not gone in, the Germans would've won a tremendous victory. But that on its own wouldn't necessarily have worried the United States. After all, they could've dealt with the Germans as the big European power. But I think they probably felt that they had to intervene to defend present and future US interests in the globe prior to the First World War. The interest of the United States was largely in its own territory, and in South America, which it called its "backyard."

The United States apparently loaned Britain quite a bit of money for World War I. The bonds totaled several billion dollars, I believe, at the time. These would not have been repaid if Germany had won the war. Would there have been an arrangement reached with Germany?

I think there were ways of reaching arrangements. But the Russian Revolution must have concentrated minds a great deal. Woodrow Wilson, as president of the United States, felt he had to come up with an alternative. And his alternative was national independence, self-determination, but also the Treaty of Versailles. So the Treaty of Versailles was pushed through by Wilson, and the punishment of Germany was directly responsible for the rise of fascism. I don't think there's any two ways about that. The way the Germans were treated gave rise to a very virulent national movement in Germany, which later became the Third Reich. All of the early propaganda of the Nazis emphasized that Germans had been dealt a rough hand: the German people are being punished, the German nation is being punished, the German race is being punished, and it's Americans, the Jewish plutocrats in New York, and their friends in Germany who are uniting against us.

This is decisive. If the Treaty of Versailles had been more evenhanded, or let us suppose that the United States had done in Europe after the First World War what it did after the Second World War—that is, to say that we are perfectly prepared to do business with you and to help you recover—who knows what it would've been like.

And if the Versailles Treaty was one element in helping the Nazis come to power, the other element was without doubt the fear of Bolshevism. That the decisions made by the top German corporations, and large numbers of the German aristocracy, which is not often recognized to have backed Hitler and have put him in power was because they were fearful that if we don't go with Hitler there's going to be a revolution in Germany.

Look what they did in Russia and we're going to be sunk, so better go with this guy who's going to save us from the Bolsheviks. The effect of the Russian Revolution was a massive rise of the German workers' movement. The split inside the German labor movement was between a pro-Bolshevik wing, and a more traditional social-democratic wing. And if you look at all the propaganda of the German nationalists and the German fascists, the threat was always presented as a Jewish Bolshevik conspiracy. So the Jews played two roles. They were either plutocrats or they were Bolsheviks. The pamphlets, the literature, was about Germany fighting against the Jewish Bolshevik conspiracy, and that went straight into the Second World War.

Was not Hitler, to some degree, popular in England? And was not Mussolini popular in the United States? And the Bank of England and the Bank of International Settlements seemed to support Hitler.

Absolutely. I was looking the other day at the first biography of Mussolini, published in Britain in 1926. The introduction was by the US ambassador to Italy, who wrote that Mussolini is one of the greatest leaders that Europe has thrown up, and this is the way to the future—largely because he was seen as a bastion against Bolshevism and revolution, much like Hitler. Winston Churchill adored Mussolini. And in that biography you'll find quotes from Churchill saying that Mussolini is a very important figure, we support him, and he's necessary. Churchill always used to spell things out. If the Bolshevik hordes are going to be held at bay, we need people like Benito Mussolini. And later during the Second World War, Mussolini threw these quotes back at Churchill, saying there was a time when the leader of the British people used to like me. What's happened? And the same with Hitler. There was a very strong element within the British ruling class that wanted to do a deal with Hitler. The British king before he abdicated, Edward VIII, was an open admirer of the Nazis, and after he abdicated, he went and called on Hitler. There are photographs of him and his wife seeing Hitler, being photographed with him. And the reason for that was the same. They said the main enemy we all confront is Bolshevism and the Russian Revolution. So anything that keeps that at bay is helpful.

The British appeasers, as they came to be known, they were extremely right-wing politicians, but they were not irrational. They said if Hitler can be turned against the Russians, that would be tremendous. Let's use him to wipe out the Soviet Union, and then we can talk. I mean, what they didn't realize is that if that had happened, the Soviet Union might well have fallen, but it would have made Hitler so powerful he would've taken Europe overnight.

If you look at France, when the Nazis marched in—the archive footage of when Hitler went to France after it had been occupied is available—you see cheering crowds greeting him in parts of France. It took some years for de Gaulle and the communists to get their act together and for the resistance to begin. But the traditional anti-Semitism of the French—and their nationalism—was the basis for the Vichy regime, and the collaboration, which most of France quite happily carried through with

Hitler. This is something that is not talked about too much but is very important to understand.

You have written about the defeat of the Russian Revolution, and you not only talk about the fifteen or sixteen armies that invaded, but about the change when Stalin took over, and what that did to the working class.

What happened in the Soviet Union was that the revolution was isolated. And it's the history of all revolutions that when they happen, there is a concert of powers that develops against them. The French found the same thing. The American Revolution had similar problems with the British. After the French Revolution toppled the monarchy and the French Republic was established, every single monarch in Europe saw this as a threat. They were trembling with fear. So you have Germans, the Russians, the English, the Austro-Hungarians trying to establish a reactionary coalition to surround and defeat the French Revolution. And at the head of it was the Prussian aristocracy, the Junkers, always there when needed. And after the Russian Revolution, the same thing happened. All the European powers tried to defeat this revolution, even though they'd just lost millions of lives fighting a crazy war, the First World War. Millions died in that war so that the European colonial powers could have more colonies or maintain their colonies. But that didn't stop them from trying to defeat the Russian Revolution at its birth. So when you had a civil war started in Russia by the supporters of the tsar, you immediately had sixteen or seventeen armies sent in by the Europeans and other foreign powers to back these people. And that civil war consumed a lot of the energy of the revolution. A lot of the best people who had made the revolution died. Less experienced people, largely rural recruits from the peasantry, were brought up, put into places of power, lacking some of the old traditions of the Russian working class. And historically, the fact is that a lot of the workers of Petrograd, who made the revolution, I think the figures are between 30 and 40 percent of them, died during the civil war, which is a very high figure indeed. And on this basis of new recruits from the countryside grew the power of the Soviet bureaucracy typified by Stalin.

There were two currents within Bolshevism. One was to say there is no way we can make socialism on our own, and so we shouldn't try it in that sense until we have support from Germany, or France, until the revolution spreads. We need that because we're a backward country. We need German industry in order to move forward. But with the defeat of the German Revolution in the 1920s, that policy was no longer active, and another current emerged that insisted you could build "socialism in one country." That was the current of Stalinism.

What year would be the defeat of the Russian Revolution?

I would say that the defeat of the hopes of the Russian Revolution was probably 1929 or 1930, when the big collectivization programs started. Collectivization was essentially an admission of defeat. And the brutality with which that collectivization was imposed on the Russian peasantry left a very deep mark in parts of the countryside, which is why when the Germans entered Ukraine, they were greeted as liberators by many Ukrainians. And if the Germans hadn't been so reactionary and so deadly, they might have had more impact, but because they regarded all Slavs as lesser peoples, they wiped them out.

Did some of these views come from King Leopold's campaign in the Belgian Congo?

The European colonial mind saw people as inferior. King Leopold, unlike other colonial leaders, actually had the Congo registered in his own name. So it wasn't Belgium that owned the Congo, it was King Leopold. It was the Belgian royal family. People talk about the six million Jews who died in the twentieth century. They never talk about the Congolese, and the figures given by Adam Hochschild in his book *King Leopold's Ghost* are that at least eleven to twelve million Congolese people were killed by the Belgians in the Congo. There was a massive genocide in that country.

Killed perhaps by their proxies, tribal warfare?

No, they were actually killed as the Belgians were trying to get the rubber plantations going. The way they treated them, the way they showed King Leopold how many people they'd killed, is all documented. They cut off their hands, or their thumbs, and sent them back in parcels to Belgium.

So the greatest enemy of the Soviet Union was perhaps England, would you say, in the postrevolutionary years?

I think England was probably the most intelligent and conscious enemy of the Russian Revolution, seeing it for the threat that it was. But the Germans weren't too far behind. I think because England was never really threatened by a revolution, the impact of the Russian Revolution in Britain was not as great as it was on the European continent. It was significant, but the reason Britain hated the Russians primarily was because the British Empire was threatened, not because they were threatened internally. Because colonized people in Africa and Asia especially saw the Russian Revolution as a gleam of hope. And the British were very panicked by that.

In 1919, in Afghanistan, a king called Amanullah, whose queen was called Soraya, was very impressed by the Russian Revolution, and opened up negotiations with Lenin asking for help against the British. Queen Soraya said we have to follow the path of Russia and Turkey, and liberate our women. So the proposed constitution of Afghanistan from this period, which was drafted in 1919, would have given women the right to vote. If that constitution had been implemented, women would have had the right to vote in Afghanistan before they did in the United States, and certainly in Europe. And then the British said that this is leading in a very bad direction, and organized a tribal revolt to get rid of that particular king and queen in Afghanistan.

The British who invaded Baku, protecting the oil fields there, were they a ferocious army? Who was responsible for the greatest amount of killing of the Russian revolutionaries?

I think it was a combination, but the British were strongly involved in killing—especially during the civil war, the early period of the revolution. The British had lost an entire generation of young men in the First World War, but that never stopped them, because they felt the stakes were very high, and that if there was a revolutionary state established there, this was going to wreck the British Empire. And the British Empire had to be preserved at all costs. What they didn't see was that the entry of the United States into the First World War was actually, if you think about it now, a very serious death blow against the British Empire. because it showed that the British on their own couldn't get their way in the world anymore. They needed the United States. They used to think: we will manipulate the United States. It's a young power, we created them, they speak our own language. We are the experienced people. We will bring them around to our way of thinking. Well, of course, the Americans privately used to laugh at that. They knew that was never going to happen.

Can you describe Woodrow Wilson's involvement in sending troops to Russia?

The United States, certainly the corporations there, saw the very existence of the Soviet Union after 1917 as a threat. Not that they feared its impact on the United States so greatly, though even there, there was an impact. Remember that it was Wilson's FBI director and attorney general who expelled large numbers of Italians from the United States, citing the supposed anarchist threat or the Bolshevik threat. People used to go knocking on doors of working-class homes of European migrants who were active in trade unions in US cities, dragging them out in the night, and expelling them. It was a panic, because there was no real threat of a massive Bolshevik party building itself in the United States. But they didn't want to take the risk. And of course, when you're panicked like that, a state panics, its leaders panic, its corporate class panics. Then they think, what can we do? Why don't we destroy the head of this serpent whose tentacles are everywhere? Go and put something in its eye, and that was Russia. So Wilson was very determined to defeat the Russian Revolution in its infancy, but he couldn't do it. And of course, the Russian Revolution then tragically defeated itself in the 1930s. But that didn't become obvious to people until the 1950s or the 1960s. So this idea that this was a real threat to the West persisted, and was, of course, the central mythology during the Cold War period—that the Russians had revolutionary aims for Europe, which is why NATO was created, which is why we had to build a massive military-industrial complex to guard and defend the United States against Russia. Well, we now know because of all the documentation that's now a matter of public record that this was nonsense.

Did the Americans achieve any destruction in Russia that you know of?

Very little. They backed the armies that went into Russia. They helped the counterrevolutionary armies during the civil war. But actually in terms of real destruction, it was minimal compared to what happened later during the Cold War. I mean, there's nothing on the level of what happened in Vietnam, or Korea, not to mention Japan right at the end of the Second World War. But also, it's important to remember that the war in the early 1920s was not what it is today. Basically, the machine gun, the Gatling gun, these were the guns which they were using, which seemed very frightening, and they were, but the weaponry was not as advanced as it is today. So those wars, though they took lives, and many people died in hospital beds because there wasn't enough medical treatment, which is why casualties were so high. Air power, for instance, was barely ever used in that period.

In Baghdad, I think in 1924, "Bomber" Harris—

"Bomber" Harris experimented in Baghdad throwing fire bombs on the Kurdish tribes. Certainly.

Can we talk about the causes of World War II overall, and the US entry into the war? You've said some interesting things about Pearl Harbor.

I think that what happened during the Second World War was, one, you had the rise of Germany as an expansionist power determined to revenge itself for the punishments of the First World

War. And when Hitler occupied France, he made that explicit. The famous archive footage of the Germans insisting that the French general surrender in the same railway coach in which the Germans had surrendered at the time of the First World War was intended to show the Germans, "We are back." This is what they did to us during the First World War. Now we have done it to them. But behind all the demagoguery, there was a fairly straightforward imperialist concern on the part of the Germans. Study the speeches of the leaders of the Third Reich closely, Hitler himself, but not just Hitler; go read Goebbels in particular, and study them seriously as political speeches without demonizing them. Just stand apart for a minute. What they are saying is this: Britain is a much smaller country than Germany, but they occupy so much of the world, as Hitler said in one of his speeches. The French, who are the French? They're much, much, much smaller than us. And look at the countries they occupy. Look at what Belgium occupies. So they should share. We've been asking them nicely to share the world with us, to share their colonies, but these guys refuse, so we're going to go in and teach them, and Germany will become a world power. So that side of the Second World War was a very traditional war between competing empires. Germany, which wanted to be an empire, and the French and the British—and the Belgians—who were empires. So that side of it was very strong. The big question was why the Germans didn't do more to keep the United States out.

So, let's talk about Pearl Harbor. Pearl Harbor, I think, had to happen sooner or later, because the Japanese felt that the United

States was putting embargos on them, pressuring them, that they had to hit back. And, you know, whether the exact details of it were known in the United States, I don't know, but I think there must've been a sigh of relief among certain sectors who wanted to break the country from isolationism. Because the isolationist current in the United States is always very strong, and was even more so after the First World War. And there is an honorable side to that, too, saying it's not our business to go and interfere in other parts of the world. Why should we? But against that, you had people who felt that US interests could only be defended by going abroad. They couldn't keep out of this. And I think there's no doubt that Roosevelt and some of the people close to him wanted to enter that war. It's sort of public knowledge now.

So the point I make about Pearl Harbor was that it was very convenient. After it happened, the whole of the United States was committed to war. And a lot of things were done in the United States that really should never have been done, like the internment of the Japanese American population, that as a result of Pearl Harbor were accepted by the population as a whole. I always wondered, you know, just as a little footnote here, if the United States had decided in the weeks that followed 9/11 that every American Muslim should be put in a camp indefinitely what the reaction would have been. I fear there would not have been much reaction. I fear that. I mean, a good few people would have raised their voices, but in any case, to return to the Second World War, they did that, and Pearl Harbor became, I mean not surprisingly, then the cause of the United States going into battle. The point is this: after the United States declared war on the kingdom of Japan, the other Axis powers, Italy and Germany, declared war on the United States. Now they needn't have done. Hitler was not told about the attack on Pearl Harbor. He could have said we were not part of this, we are not declaring war on the United States. Yet he did. And I think it was a rash move, because some people in the United States would've argued, let's concentrate now on wiping out Japan, let's go straight into the Pacific, let's not deal with the Germans.

Isn't it remarkable that, in November 1940, Roosevelt is elected on a platform of not going into the war? This is after England is under serious attack and is in jeopardy of falling. Many people have suggested that Roosevelt felt that England would fall.

Yes.

So he would be willing to give away—

England.

Europe?

I think so. And I think it was not only him. To be fair to Roosevelt, most people thought England wouldn't survive.

If that's the case, then I would think Roosevelt is thinking about a future world without England as controlling all these colonies. Would these colonies perhaps become available to Roosevelt?

Absolutely. I think that this was a big point of discussion within the United States ruling elite: the British Empire is collapsing, and we will have to take it over, as much as we can, in order to preserve and protect our own global interests. In one message to Churchill, Roosevelt said it would be a big tragedy if the British Navy fell into the hands of the Germans, so I suggest you send your entire navy to US ports so we can look after it for you. And Churchill was horrified, because the idea of defeat didn't enter into the equation for him.

So the Atlantic Charter, the meeting in Newfoundland, plays a serious role here because Churchill comes over in early 1941, and makes a deal, so to speak, with Roosevelt, to defend what they called the Four Freedoms?

I think by that time the British had survived. It became clearer in 1941 that they were going to fight on. The Battle of Britain had taken place in the air, and hadn't been followed by a German invasion of Britain. That's the other interesting thing. The Germans stepped back when England was ready actually for the plucking.

And go instead to Russia.

Hitler decided that he had to go against Russia, and they began to plan Operation Barbarossa, another big strategic error made by the Germans. Just thinking from their point of view, either you go for Russia in the beginning and deal with it, and that's what some of their generals were advising; or, if you've started to pulverize Britain, because you want the British Empire, then go for it. But at the last minute they changed their mind. So there was a lot of irrationality there.

Coming back to Roosevelt, I think once Britain had survived that initial German onslaught, he thought probably these guys are going to make it, and we have to do something now. But the fact that he came to power on a pacifist ticket, saying we're not going to go into any wars, is an indication on how deep that pacifist isolationist feeling ran inside the United States.

Let's follow the money for a moment. We know that many Americans are tied to Germany by birth, and we know there's a lot of money in Germany. We know that perhaps we can make a deal with the Germans financially that could be lucrative. Bonds and stocks can be traded with Germany, as well as with Britain, but there's a strong anti-British feeling in America.

There is, and I mean, Henry Ford, you know, one of the sort of great industrialists of the United States was very pro-German, did his deals with them, as did others.

And Charles Lindbergh.

And Lindbergh. And so, you know, the thing for them, I mean just thinking purely as captains of industry, capitalism essentially is color blind, gender blind. It's a struggle for profits. And so why privilege Britain rather than Germany? That's how they thought. And the fact that Germany had an anticommunist leadership, that was fine. In fact, it was even good.

To follow the money further, I wonder about Pearl Harbor. If you study the Japanese aggression from 1931 onward in China, Japan is clearly dying for empire, an Asian sphere, throwing out the white man, throwing out the foreigners. So Japan is seriously pursuing wealth, chopping up China, going toward Thailand and Indochina, Indonesia, the oil-producing crescent of South Asia. Japan is growing very rich, right? So why is America all of a sudden putting an embargo on Japan at that point? Why are they stopping the Japanese from getting rich at the same time that they are defending the interests of the British and French Empires in South Asia?

I think a significant proportion of leaders in the United States felt that it would be easier for them to take over the role of the British globally than it would be to take colonies away from the French or the Japanese. I mean, that was a tradition. That if it's the Brits, if this falls totally into the hands of the Japanese, it's lost to us forever, or for a long time to come. Whereas if it's in the hands of the British or the French—

Or the Germans—

Or the Dutch, then it becomes much, much easier.

So they would trust the Germans more than Japanese because of racial considerations?

The racial thing was so strong that I think young people in the United States would be genuinely shocked were they to look back at the propaganda images of the war against Japan. Regardless of what Japan had done, the so-called yellow peril, the vicious portrayal of the Japanese in US propaganda as "yellow devils" went very deep indeed. And we know that racism has played a very strong part in the United States. People sometimes forget that the Ku Klux Klan wasn't just a tiny group of idiots who went around dressed in white, lynching Black people, but was probably one of the largest political movements this country has ever had with millions and millions of members. It was a genuine, popular, mass movement of poor whites. That is a reality. And so playing to that audience in the United States was very easy. And, of course, there had already been restrictions on migration of Chinese workers into the United States itself. So it went very deep.

An embargo is serious. An American embargo is the declaration of war, so to speak.

It was.

Like our Cuban blockade.

Yes, it was serious.

And the Japanese I think decided they had to either take on the United States now or never.

I think you're right. The other choice they had, of course, if they'd been thinking strategically, is to have attacked Russia, which made much more sense from their point of view, and then they could've linked up with their German comrades halfway between and occupied Russia. Instead they decided to hit the United States, which immediately brought the United States into the war. And that was ultimately that.

There seems to have been a lack of coordination between Japan and Germany. That's astounding on many fronts.

It is astounding.

Especially in the Russian situation because the Japanese withdrew from Siberia in about 1940, I think, and they moved the Russian general Zhukov from Siberia to Stalingrad.

Once Russian intelligence concluded that the Japanese had decided not to invade the Soviet Union, they could move all their troops and throw them into battle against the Germans. One of the top spies the Russians had, a very, very brilliant old Bolshevik spy, Richard Zorga, came from an old German family of Bolsheviks and fled to Russia. He spoke perfect German, looked like a perfect Aryan. He was based in Japan, and was so close to the German embassy in Tokyo that when the ambassador went back to Berlin, Zorga virtually ran the embassy. So he saw all the reports. And he warned the Russians, he warned Stalin, that the Germans are preparing to invade Russia. He sent them the planned date of Operation Barbarossa (though Stalin didn't believe him). So Russian intelligence in Japan was very good. And the minute they knew Japan isn't attacking us, all the troops were thrown into battle against the Germans.

Could it have been that Hitler was very confident that Russia would be his and that he didn't want the Japanese coming in the back door and taking part of his treasure?

It could well be, actually.

And would Germany have gone on to smash the Japanese if they had won?

I think they would have done a deal. You know, you keep the Greater Japanese Empire, but keep it to the east, and we will run Europe and Greater Russia.

What were the Germans thinking about the United States in all this? Do we know?

They thought they would make a deal with the United States. They were absolutely convinced of this, precisely because of what you said about the large German American population. And so the hostility to the United States wasn't so great, which is why in all the propaganda used by the Third Reich against the United States, they used to say that the problem with the United States is the plutocracy, and the Jewish wing of that plu-tocracy, which is going to drag the United States into war; that Roosevelt is a prisoner of the Jewish plutocracy, because they couldn't bring themselves to attack a country in which a large section of the population came from Germany.

Chapter 2

The Post–World War II Order

Oliver Stone: You've written that the self-sufficiency in essential raw materials that characterized the United States came to an end after the Second World War. The United States found it needed to import oil, iron ore, bauxite, copper, manganese, nickel, oil. Can you talk a bit about the US need for raw materials after World War II and what happened after it had become the richest country in the world?

Tariq Ali: After the war, people's expectations were much higher than they had been in earlier periods. The manufacture of cars, for instance, the explosion of that particular industry, the explosion of the military-industrial complex, was on the scale that no American leader could have conceived of prior to the First World War. So they were making sure that they were never short of supplies in order to keep the country going, and in order to protect and preserve US imperial interests, especially oil. So they needed raw materials. Eisenhower actually once even spoke in terms of the importance of Vietnam in terms of the raw materials the United States needed. And the deal with Saudi Arabia, which later came to haunt the United States in the twenty-first century, was very interesting because it showed the transition from one empire to another before the first empire had officially collapsed. The United States took over the role of guarding the Saudi royal family and all their interests from the British during the Second World War. The meeting where this took place was on a boat, a special boat in the Suez Canal. That's where the deal was signed.

Protect the family from who?

To protect the family from its own people.

Even then?

Even then. The Saudi royal family, and especially the brand of religion that it believed in, the Wahabi faith, represented a tiny number of people in Saudi Arabia. So they used the strength they gained first from their deals with the British Empire and subsequently with the United States in order to preserve their stranglehold over their own people and to impose this particular religion on the people in Saudi Arabia, who really didn't share it. So that goes back to the Second World War. But increasingly the

United States was thinking, even while the war was going on, the French have collapsed, what is happening to the French colonies? The Dutch can't fight, they're occupied by the Germans. What's going to happen in Indonesia? What is going to happen in Indochina? What is going to happen to India? Can we let the Japanese take India? Because at one point there was a real danger.

Can you talk about that briefly?

After the fall of Singapore in 1942, the Indian nationalists, Gandhi in particular, and Nehru, felt that they might end up discussing Indian independence, not with the British, but with the Japanese. So for the first time Gandhi made a strategic error, or a tactical error. He said, let us call on the British to leave India now. And the British said to him, wait until the war is over. We're going to go. He said, no, you have to go now. So they withdrew all their people from governments within Indian provinces, and waged a civil disobedience movement called Quit India. Now people see this just as a national movement, which it was, but it was linked to the big Japanese offensive after the fall of Singapore, which was seen as the biggest defeat for the British military in Asia. And the British felt the Japanese are moving on, they're reaching Burma. Soon they will occupy Bengal. And after they occupy Bengal, well, who knows? They might take Delhi. So the British government, Churchill in particular, panicked and sent left-wing politicians from Britain to see Gandhi, and say to him, look, we'll give you whatever you want, but just hang on a bit. We're giving you a blank check. And Gandhi replied, what is the point of a blank check from a bank that is failing? He really thought that the Brits were finished. But of course, the Japanese never made it to Delhi, though it is worth remembering that lots of Indian soldiers captured by the Japanese were transformed into an Indian national army. And there was one central leader of the Indian Congress Party, Subhas Chandra Bose, who flew to Tokyo and Berlin on the nationalist slogan "the enemy of my enemy is my friend," and did deals with Hitler and the Japanese to launch a military offensive within India against the British. This was the Indian National Army, which was very popular.

What happened?

They didn't get very far. They did fight against the British. Many of them were arrested. And after the war, when they were being brought to trial, top Indian politicians, including Nehru, donned their lawyers' clothes and went in to defend them, saying they were nationalist patriots. We didn't agree with them, but they did what they did against a country that was occupying them.

Since Japan had Burma, why didn't they send more troops over to India?

It is another of these mysteries, why they gave up on India, why they didn't invade the Soviet Union. They just gave up at one point in time, and felt that they had to concentrate everything elsewhere. I think, by that time, they probably felt that their supply lines were a bit overstretched.

Did India have any wealth for Japan?

Well, India had enormous wealth, potential wealth.

Potential, but not at the moment.

Not at the moment. It was wealth which would have to be exploited, but they had a massive labor force.

Yes, but they would've had to be fed, and the Japanese did have food problems.
You've written that, after the Second World War, essentially the United States struck a deal with Japan to run a form of one-party state, am I correct?

People talk a great deal about General MacArthur writing the Japanese constitution. When the United States invaded Iraq in 2003, people proposed a "Japanese-style" occupation of Iraq. But the occupation of Japan was by no means progressive. First, why keep the Japanese emperor around? Normally the United States did not have too much time for that, nor did the French because of their republican traditions. Rule through monarchs is more of a British tradition. But in the case of Japan, I think MacArthur and the US government decided that removing the emperor from the throne of Japan and making Japan a republic might unleash social and political forces in the country that they couldn't control. They always needed people to control these countries on their behalf, and they felt they stood a better chance with the emperor. In fact, the astonishing thing is that the emperor was already preparing the speech he expected to make when he was tried as a war criminal, because he was centrally involved in the war. And when MacArthur went to see him, he thought this was the end. In fact, MacArthur said, hang on, we're keeping you on, your position is safe.

The other thing to bear in mind is that, after the Second World War, in all three Axis countries, Japan, Germany, Italy, the bulk of the military structure of these countries was kept intact, and the same personnel who had fought against the United States continued to play prominent roles. In Japan, for example, they removed very few people. There was a war crimes tribunal to prosecute Tojo and some others, but by and large they kept the army in force. In Italy, 60 to 65 percent of Mussolini's structure in the judiciary, in the military, in the police force was kept in place. In Germany, you probably have the biggest purge, but still a lot of former Nazis joined the Christian Democratic Party, and played a part in the police force and the judiciary, because by this time, the enemy was communism. And so anything that could be used against the communists was used.

Was there a moment during the Second World War when the United States became an imperial power of the magnitude to inherit the British mantle?

From the moment it began, really, something had to give. If the First World War was a decisive event for making the United States a world power, bringing it onto the world stage, the Second World War was a decisive event in terms of making the United States an imperial power, which meant it had to fight wars to preserve its dominion. This soon led to the interventions in Korea, in Vietnam, and so on. Of course, the United States had always been an empire in North America, as we know, expanding its territory at the expense of Mexico. Buying Louisiana from the French, kicking the Brits out. Controlling South America indirectly, by and large, even though the marines went in time and time again, as General Smedley Butler reminds us in his wonderful book *War Is a Racket*. By and large, the way the United States preferred to rule the world was to find local relays who would do their bidding. Where they did intervene directly, the results weren't always happy, like in the Philippines.

You have pointed out that Britain ruled India with only, I think, thirty thousand soldiers.

That is amazing, yes. At the height of the British rule in India, there were thirty-six thousand white English soldiers. But the Brits, because they decided to stay there, ruled this vast and populous subcontinent by doing deals with wings of its ruling class in different parts, and creating a "new model army," the British Indian Army, which was staffed with people from the poorest sections of the Indian countryside. They avoided recruiting in the towns, recruiting mainly poor peasants, or mountain people, like the Gurkhas, instead, who were paid and looked after. It was a sort of paternalistic army. They troops weren't just left to rot, and that was a very successful operation, which no imperial power could ever repeat again.

And they developed a landlord class?

They did indeed. In previous centuries, during the Mughal empire, landlordism hadn't been encouraged. The state was dominant. The British created a class of landlords by giving larger states to people who were already notables in these regions but who exercised power through collecting taxes, rather than ownership of land, though in many cases they had slowly begun to accumulate landholdings. So the British institutionalized all this by saying to these people, you're the landlords, you control these areas, you control the tenants under you, and we need your support. A lot of tenants from these estates often went and fought for the British army in China, in Indochina, and elsewhere in the world. Lots of Indian soldiers died in the Second World War in the fields of Europe.

So you're saying the United States inherited, with certain exceptions, this colonial legacy?

They inherited this colonial legacy from the British, but they didn't operate the way the British did. When the British occupied Africa, British civil servants were stationed around the country. The queen was the head of the country. I mean, it was a traditional, old-fashioned colonialism. If you were a French colony in Africa, you were part of the French commonwealth. All the deals were essentially done in Paris. The United States didn't go down that route. One reason they didn't is because the early ideology of the United States was we are an anticolonial country because we had to get rid of a colonial power, the Brits, ourselves. And this played a very important part in how the United States formulated its thinking about its own empire. They could never admit they were an empire. It is only recently, since the collapse of the Soviet Union, that they've begun to do that. And so that played some part in it, and that didn't encourage them to send Americans around to staff the customs service of country X or country Y. They've always been unhappy when they're forced to do that, as in Iraq today. So it was a different type of an empire. As a matter of fact, the British got more financially out of controlling Argentina indirectly than they got out of occupying Africa. And for the United States, I think it is this financial aspect that is paramount when US interests are concerned—what their corporations can do, what is the best possible atmosphere for them to function. That has dominated US thinking for a long time.

More of a neoliberal, free-market philosophy?

Much more of that, even before these words were invented. That is how the United States has tended to operate. I mean, that is how they built up the Saudi oil industry. ARAMCO went in, and actually built the oil industry in Saudi Arabia, which the Saudis later took over with very handsome compensation, and permanent tribute basically to Washington. US companies would go in, personnel attached to their companies would go in, intelligence agents would go in to keep Washington informed of what was going on, but they didn't like direct occupations or sending in troops unless it became absolutely necessary.

You've observed that England was very clever in using the antislavery platform to colonize Africa.

It's quite interesting that the argument the British gave for the colonization of Africa, and for sending British troops, was that this is the only way we can end slavery, ignoring the fact that Britain and fortunes had been made in Britain from the slave trade for many, many decades. But that was the argument they used, and I compare it to the argument used by the United States that we're taking this country or that country to defend human rights. These are ideological justifications, given largely to their own people at home, to make something that is unseemly more palatable. But the British were the cheekiest, actually.

Would slavery have ended otherwise, or did the British actually end it?

No, slavery was coming to an end, more or less. The process had begun in the nineteenth century, especially after the defeat of the South in the American Civil War. And in Europe, it was ending. The French Revolution had ended it. The Haitian slaves had revolted. So what the British said was very typical of British imperialism, a lot of bogus, hypocritical talk. The way they ruled Africa was totally racist. I mean, if you look at what they did when they ruled Africa, they imposed an apartheid system on the country. They built whites-only clubs, whites-only segregated areas. People say the Afrikaners did that in South Africa, but the British did it all over the world, in India as well, but largely in Africa.

I'd be curious, what do you think of Dr. Livingston, the Scottish missionary doctor?

Once you belong to an imperial country, an imperial race, you think the world is yours. And even good people, you know, they decide that they can go and explore the world, and discover things. In the back of their mind is the fact that we are the empire, everything I'm doing is for the empire. And Livingston was not immune to that. The Scottish are now very hostile to the English. But in terms of the British Empire, the Scotts sometimes tended to be the most die-hard imperialists. They played a big role in establishing the British Empire, and in administering it.

And there was a religious component, too. That was always part of it. We are bringing civilization and the Christian religion to the heathens. We will help them, but in return they have to become Christians. A lot of the missionaries believed that, and they believed it quite genuinely without any bad motives. In order to save these souls, we have to make sure the body is kept alive, too. The Brits did it in Australia to a certain extent, as well, converting the Aboriginals, bringing them to our way of life. And, of course, most of them were wiped out.

Would Sir Richard Burton be on your bad-guy list?

Well, Burton was a very interesting guy, and my bad-guy list isn't so big, you know. I mean, there were lots of British scholars who went out into the world and did good things, discovered languages, wrote about them. Some of these individuals were

Orientalists in the best sense of the word, that they wanted to learn about "Oriental" culture, learn the languages, translate them into English. And, for me, it is always a good thing when you begin to learn what other people are thinking. The early scholars who went to China provide us with insights into what fiction was being written in China in the eleventh century, for example, which we would never know otherwise. So, for me, these are, by and large, good guys.

Could you discuss your views of Franklin Delano Roosevelt?

Roosevelt was, I think, probably one of the most intelligent presidents produced by the United States in the twentieth century. When he decided something had to be done, he did it. He surrounded himself with very good people, strong-minded people, some of whom he trusted, some he didn't, but by and large he took a decision and pushed it through. Whether or not you agree with the particular decision, that's what he did. He was helped by the fact that, at the time of the Great Depression, the United States also had a strong labor movement. Today it's difficult to think about trade unions playing a big part in national public life in the United States, but they did at the time. There were factory occupations taking place in Flint, Michigan, where autoworkers were occupying their factories, and women were setting up the women's auxiliary, helping the strike, taking food for their men, building solidarity. And this pressure from below enabled Roosevelt to take on the giant corporations when he did, and pushed through the New Deal, which was essentially a social-democratic program for the United States. He couldn't have done this at a different time. He had this ability to communicate with people through the wireless, before the age of television, and became an effective war leader.

Howard Zinn seems to think less of Roosevelt, seeing him more as a capitalist front man who was preserving a decayed system.

This is true on one level of course, but one can say this about every politician in the Western world. Sometimes people ask me questions about Obama. And I say, well, if you wear Caesar's clothes, and you sit on Caesar's thrown, you have to behave like Caesar. But there are choices even in how to be Caesar. You can be Caligula, or you can be Claudius. You can be Constantine, or you can be Julian. So you can say that about all politicians. They are capitalists, they serve capitalist interests, and it is true. But when there are no other alternatives, then you're a bit stuck. So the question is: were there any big alternatives for Roosevelt? Looking back on the history of the twentieth century, at that point in time, Roosevelt was probably the best the United States could get. And his vice president, Henry Wallace, was a genuinely progressive soul, with genuinely radical ideas. And Roosevelt hung onto him until he was too ill and sick to fight the elements of his own party that wanted to get rid of Wallace. And the Democrats put in Harry Truman. I mean, what if Wallace had become president after Roosevelt died? Who knows how the Cold War would have unfolded, whether it would have started in that particular way or not, or whether Wallace would have used nuclear weapons against Japan.

Would Roosevelt have used nuclear weapons?

That's an interesting question. I think there was a side of him that reflected the common views in the United States about the Japanese. That was not his strong point, Japan.

He came to accept terror bombing, it seems.

He did. You know, the terror bombing that took place in German towns—Dresden, and so on—was it militarily necessary? I don't think so. But once you accept that, then the jump from the terror bombing of Dresden and Hamburg to using and testing these new weapons in Japan is not a big leap. I always wonder whether they would've tested these weapons out on a white race. Let's put it bluntly. Somehow the Japanese had been demonized so much that wiping out two whole cities didn't really matter. Everyone agreed to it. It wasn't just the Americans. The British agreed, the Russians agreed to it. Left-wing—

You say the Russians agreed to it?

The Russians agreed to it.

To Hiroshima?

Stalin agreed to it. Even though it was a shot across their own bow, the Russians were informed that these weapons were going to be tested on Japan and they didn't protest.

Postwar anticommunism took root more in the United States than in France or other parts of Europe. What was the reason behind that?

I think in France, of course, you had a large resistance during the Second World War. And there were two components of that resistance. There was a nationalist resistance under General de Gaulle. He was greatly admired because he had stood firm when France fell, and said we will fight these guys until the end. Then, after the Soviet Union was attacked—and only after then—did the French Communist Party throw itself heart and soul into the resistance, and they lost many, many people. So the traditions of that resistance remained very strong in France right until the 1980s. And the communist role in that resistance meant that it wasn't easy to vilify or demonize them. And the French intelligentsia that grew up in that particular period, whether they were members of the Communist Party or not, were in general sympathetic to Marxist ideas. I talk particularly of Jean-Paul Sartre, Simone de Beauvoir, the whole school of younger people around them and *Les Temps modernes*, the magazine they set up. In addition, you had with de Gaulle a president who, in later years of the Cold War, didn't want to be part of the American plans for global domination. He took France out of NATO, and he opposed the war in Vietnam. He came to Montreal, not far from the United States and said, "Vive le Québec libre!" You know, what more could he do? So that meant that France was never part of the Cold War ideology in the same way as the United States.

McCarthyism in that exact form in which it formed in the United States couldn't have been found in too many countries in Europe, Scandinavia excluded. Italy had a giant communist party, largely because of the role it had played in the resistance.

Yet in the United States we had numerous strikes during World War II, and the question is why we changed so abruptly from 1944 to 1947, when Truman signed the antilabor Taft-Hartley law? Looking back, Eugene Debs ran for president, and he ends up in jail. Big Bill Haywood ends up running away from America because he's sentenced to jail. It seems that we broke the back of the labor unions with Emma Goldman's deportation and the Palmer Raids. There seems to be an ongoing war against labor.

There was a total war against the American labor movement, especially from the beginning from the 1920s onward. And if you look at the statistics of the number of physical attacks on striking workers, either by the police or by private companies and goons hired by the corporations, it's quite astonishing. Repression backed by the state, or accepted by the state, was used to crush a labor movement in this country. In this time, the "Bolshevik threat" played a very big part, too. And it's at this same time that US leaders began to use religious imagery. The motto "In God We Trust" was put on the dollar in the 1950s. And increasingly presidents who were not deeply religious started paying lip service to religion. Why? Because religion was seen as a weapon against communism. And the state began to use religious emblems, as well. That is quite an interesting feature of the Cold War, which has led us partially where we are today. The United States has become a much more religious country than it used to be, with religion being taken far more seriously. Before the Cold War, religion was a sort of private matter; it didn't really enter into the functioning of the life of the state.

But instead of Wallace as president, we had Truman.

The removal of Henry Wallace and the election of Harry Truman meant that the United States had decided to embark on a certain course. That course was an aggressive foreign policy, taking on the Russians. The first big outbreak as a consequence of this was the Korean War. With the defeat of the Japanese, Korea became vulnerable to nationalism, to communism, to radical currents. Had the United States not intervened, there is very little doubt that the whole of the peninsula would have fallen to the communists, who interestingly were more popular in what is now South Korea than what is now North Korea. In Seoul, for example, you had much more genuine popular support for the Korean communists. Kim Il-sung didn't like many of the communists of Seoul because they reminded him of a period when communism was genuinely popular, and he didn't like to be reminded of that. So a lot of communists from the South were repressed by Kim Il-sung when he established this parody of a Stalinist dictatorship in North Korea, the Democratic People's Republic of Korea. Many communists from the South were not given positions. Many were killed, some were imprisoned.

So, the United States decided that it wasn't going to allow Korea to "fall" to communism. The United States had sent troops into Korea and a border had been established on the forty-ninth parallel between North and South Korea. The North Koreans then decided on a raid, and crossed the border, which gave the United States a pretext for a war. This war went on for three years. It was the first of the hot wars of the Cold War. And had the Chinese armies not entered, North Korea would have fallen to MacArthur. MacArthur had started saying we are going to win against the communists of North Korea, and if necessary we'll cross the Yalu River and go into China. This sort of talk was very dangerous. The Chinese Revolution had succeeded in October 1949. We talked earlier about the wave of enthusiasm for the Russian Revolution in Europe. There was a similar wave of enthusiasm for the Chinese Revolution in Asia—the Chinese way, the Chinese path. Mao Zedong was a popular hero. They had taken the world's largest country, not a small thing. So when the Korean War began, the Chinese decided we can't allow North Korea to fall, and sent in Chinese. The Chinese army fought the United States to a standstill, ultimately leading to an armistice in 1953. But it produced a lot of casualties. Mao Zedong's son died fighting in the Korean War. So that was the first of these wars. The early period of the Cold War saw the breakup of old empires, with the United States essentially increasingly taking over the role of these empires. The Korean War, the breakup of the Japanese Empire. The Vietnam War, the breakup of the French Empire.

Iran.

Events in Iran in the early 1950s showed the weakness of the British, who could no longer control Iran. The election of a nationalist government in Iran, the National Front Party, a very democratic movement led by Mohammed Mosaddegh, was a turning point. The first thing Mosaddegh did when he was elected in Iran was nationalize the oil. He said Iranian oil is not going to remain under the control of the British. And at that point the United States decided to back the British, so the CIA and British intelligence organized the toppling of the Mosaddegh regime, bringing the shah back, who had fled, to Iran, and mobilizing religious people. All the demonstrations in Tehran against Mosaddegh were organized in the mosques. And with the shah in power, and all other political parties banned, torture used regularly as a weapon, the only space that could be used was the mosque.

The toppling of Mosaddegh in 1953 in Iran was part of a wider pattern. In Latin America, all attempts by South American nationalist leaders, such as Arbenz in Guatemala, to break away from Washington's embrace, from US corporations, to defend their own countries, to favor poor people, was seen as a communist outrage. The US response was to use any means available to topple them, get rid of them. We have to do virtually anything, including fighting wars, to preserve US power in these domains. And if it means linking up with the worst elements in

South America, or Iran, or Asia, we will do it. We have one enemy, communism, and everything we use against that enemy is justified. This was also the period of the Vietnam War, the most striking manifestation of that impulse. It is important to remember about the Vietnam War that it escalated soon after a big American victory in Indonesia, when they organized a coup in 1965 that wiped out one million communists, ousting the independent nationalist leader Sukarno and imposing the brutal dictator Suharto. *Time* magazine openly said this is a big, big victory for the United States—and it was.

But the Vietnam War produced its own contradictions. This was a war without end, and a war fought by conscripts, and that conscript army represented what the United States was in the 1960s. A revolt within the army began to erupt when Black and white GIs said, "Hell, no, we won't go." We ain't gonna fight in Vietnam. The Pentagon was defeated. They knew they could no longer persecute this war because they had lost the confidence of their own soldiers. The antiwar movement was very important. I would never begrudge that. But the spreading of the revolt inside the ranks of the US Army, the GIs against the war, I thought was absolutely fundamental. And there is no other event quite like that in the history of the United States, or in the history of most other nations. You have to go back to the First World War and the Russian Revolution, which happened in part because the soldiers threw down their guns and revolted. The big demonstration by GIs outside the Pentagon was quite incredible. These are soldiers in uniform on their crutches with their medals, some of the most decorated soldiers in US history, saying, we don't want to win this war, and we don't want you to prosecute this war. Unheard of. And that showed the best face of the United States. And whenever I argue with religious fundamentalists, I say basically you guys have no idea what the United States is because this is a country whose leaders are largely frightened of its own people and no one else. So you have to understand what the American citizens are, what motivates them, how they think. They brought the Vietnam War to a halt—obviously helped by the Vietnamese—which is why I think they will never have a conscript army again. That they have understood. We can't fight wars with conscript armies.

What was the relationship between Sukarno and the Non-Aligned Movement? Was that why he was seen as such a threat to the United States?

Well, the United States, as we've been discussing, believed the world was black and white. They never thought there could be gray, a leadership that was neither communist nor pro-US. The Indian government, which started Non-Alignment under Nehru, Tito in Yugoslavia, Nkrumah in Ghana, Sukarno in Indonesia, who all said, look, we don't want to be part of the Cold War. You know, we're not communists, but we don't agree with what you're doing. And a rational government in the United States would have said it's not such a bad thing to have some space between us and the communists, to have a general third way of people trying to promote their own path. But, no, the hysteria of that period was such that anyone who said we're not on their side, but we're not on your side either, was treated as an enemy. So they toppled government after government. In Indonesia, Sukarno was seen as an enemy because he would hop on a plane and go and see the Chinese. He would talk to the Vietnamese. He spoke out against the war in Vietnam. So he had to be toppled.

Suharto, as we know, was working very closely with the United States, and began to prepare a coup d'état. In the preparation of a coup d'état they usually have a provocation. Some event happens, which is seen as a provocation, and then the military strikes. They organized that pretext in Indonesia, and the military struck. They were totally prepared. Sukarno was put under house arrest. The entire Communist Party leadership was arrested. They had lists. Vigilantes were set up, mainly Islamist fundamentalist vigilantes, who went from house to house on the beautiful island of Bali, saying, that's a communist family living in that house, bring them out, kill the women.

There were lists provided by—

—The CIA and the local intelligence. One of the things the CIA used to do in every country, as Philip Agee informed us, was to prepare lists of the subversives, the communists, the guerrillas. Often they compiled these names by grabbing people and torturing them. In Iraq, they worked with people inside the Baath Party, such as Saddam Hussein, who supplied them with the lists of communists to wipe out, which Hussein did. Similar lists were provided to Suharto.

Many of the people killed in Indonesia in 1965 were Chinese, am I right?

And many of the poorest—

Was there a racial component to this?

Well, after the victory of the Chinese Revolution, many of the local Chinese were very sympathetic to the revolution, and that made them sympathetic to the Indonesian Communist Party. So in Jakarta, and places where you had a large Chinese population, even in Vietnam; by the way, in Saigon, the United States utilized this fact to encourage xenophobia toward Chinese minorities. They'd say, we are defending South Vietnamese interests against the Chinese who live in Cholon, or we are defending the Indonesian interests against these wicked evil foreign Chinese. But the main objective was to wipe out the Indonesian Communist Party as a political force. This was the largest Communist Party in the world outside the official communist countries. And Indonesia was the largest Muslim country in the world. When they wiped the party out, they created a big political vacuum.

One million people were killed?

One million people.

Men, women, children?

Men, women, children. And the descriptions of that are horrendous—

Across the whole country?

Across the whole country, in villages, including this idyllic island of Bali, where communists were quite strong. I've read the most horrendous descriptions of these massacres. The men who were killed were disemboweled, and their genitals were hung out on display in certain areas to create fear. There were descriptions of the rivers running red with blood for days, packed with corpses.

And this was viewed by the United States, the CIA, and the government as a great victory at the time?

This was regarded by the United States as a tremendous victory because empires historically tend to be very short-term in their thinking. They rarely think ahead strategically.

If they're willing to dispense with Sukarno, who is a major non-aligned leader, why weren't they willing to go after Nehru in India?

They were not prepared to go after Jawaharlal Nehru in India because India was a country that commanded a lot of respect in those days, particularly throughout the Western world and especially by the Europeans. Nehru was seen as a sort of social-democratic leader. He was elected, there was an opposition, and the Indian army was independent. It would have been very difficult for the United States to manipulate the Indian army. So they couldn't do anything about India, but what they could do was transform Pakistan into a US base in October 1958, by organizing a coup d'état and making the Pakistani military heavily dependant on them. Links between the Pakistani military and the Pentagon date back to the 1950s, to the Cold War period, when the ruling elites used the military to prevent a general election from taking place that they were fearful might produce a government that would take Pakistan out of all the US security pacts. The United States knew they couldn't do much about India, so they concentrated on Pakistan.

Pakistan becomes a key component in our Southeast Asia Treaty Organization.

Yes, and the Pakistani military henceforth becomes a very valued asset of the United States, with direct links to the Pentagon. Large numbers of Pakistani officers are sent for training to Fort Bragg and other American military academies. And links are established between the Pakistani military in the United States to create a special commando unit inside the Pakistani army for emergency actions. And the Indians know all this.

Who was a political threat in Pakistan at this point?

There was no immediate individual leader as a threat, but you had political parties in both West Pakistan and East Pakistan

whose manifesto said we will take Pakistan out of the US security pacts if we win the election scheduled for April 1959. We
should be a non-aligned country like India. And that was the
fear. A totally crazy fear in many ways, but it was the fear.

**Your own life was marked by coup in 1958, was it not? You
were fifteen then. Were you still in Pakistan at the time?**

Yes.

Your life could not be the same again.

It wasn't the same again. It was changed. We were very angry.
And I was very active against the military leadership. We were
organizing study circles and cells on campuses. I also organized
the first demonstration of the time. When the military takes over,
all political parties and trade unions are banned, all public
demonstrations, all public gatherings of more than four people
are not allowed. And once news came through to us, I think it
was 1961, that Patrice Lumumba, the leader of Congo, had been
killed—by the Belgians, or by the United States, or by both, we
didn't know—Nehru in India said this is the biggest crime of
all, the West will pay for this crime, having killed an independence leader. But our government remained silent. So at my university I said we have to have a meeting on the campus to defend
Lumumba and demand something. So we put our little leaflets
all over the campuses saying Patrice Lumumba is dead. Half the
students didn't know who he was, but we explained it to them,

and we had about five hundred students who assembled in this big hall. I spoke and said, look, Congo has produced its first independent leader, and they've killed him because they found him a threat. We can't sit still, so let's go out onto the streets. So they said, let's. And so we marched, we just marched out of the university to the US consulate general and said, you know, who killed Lumumba? We want answers. "Long live Lumumba!" The police were totally taken by surprise. This was the first public demonstration, defying all the military law. And then, on the way back from the US consulate in Lahore, as we approached our college, the first slogans we chanted were "death to the military dictatorship, down with the military"—and nothing happened to us. So Lumumba's assassination was one of the things that then triggered a big student movement in the country.

When did you leave Pakistan? You're now basically in exile?

I live in London. I came to study at Oxford in 1963, and then I wasn't allowed back by two different Pakistani dictators. I became an exile.

So 1958 to 1965 is a defining period if your life, and you're cut off from your roots.

I was nineteen when I came to study at Oxford.

I was around sixteen when Kennedy was killed in the same year, 1963. I think that was a turning point for me, too, because

I don't think I would've gone to Vietnam if Kennedy had been in office.

Well, that war might not have developed to that extent.

I don't think it's possible.

These things are formative.

And in the same sense I don't think that Roosevelt would have dropped the bombs on Hiroshima and Nagasaki, but that's speculation. Certainly Wallace would not have.

Wallace certainly wouldn't have dropped the atomic bomb. So, these events which happen do change people's lives. They've changed our lives, and they've changed the lives of millions.

I was on the colonialist side of the picture. I was in New York City. I didn't have any concept of what we were doing around the world in your country, in Pakistan. We were interfering in all these countries, and your life—it's your life—would be different now. Perhaps it's been improved by the turbulence and exile, and the social movement was created. But if you had been born in Indonesia, you would've had the same issue. Your life would've been like an earthquake.

Well, if I'd been born in Indonesia, and I had the same political views, I'd be dead.

An entire generation of people were shaken by US policy.

Including American citizens. Let's go back to the Vietnam War. That was probably the most formative event for an entire generation. It changed people, even people who supported the war, and many who fought in it, it changed them forever. They couldn't be the same again. I mean, it made them think. And it brought about this shift that the United States would never be able to fight a conscript war again, because if you conscript people, it affects the whole country. So the war in Iraq is a war is later fought largely by a voluntary army and mercenaries recruited from abroad.

It's ironic. The British Empire has been perhaps the most influential in terms of culture in Pakistan. You speak with an English accent. But, in reality, the American Empire is the one that changed your life by trying to determine politics in your country.

It's absolutely true. I find it difficult to imagine what life would have been like in Pakistan had there not been a military coup, had that first general election taken place. Would Pakistan have split up in 1971? It's one of those interesting counterfactuals that will remain with us forever. I mean, you know, these counterfactuals sort of intrigue me more and more. The older you become, the more you think of how these moments in history have changed your life and those of others.

We don't think about this when we're young.

No, when we're young, we don't think about these things. You know, you're prepared to do anything. I remember when I was in North Vietnam during the war, and the bombs were dropping on us every day, I just said once to the Vietnamese, we feel really bad. You know, I'm in my twenties. Can't we do something to help you? Can we help man the anti-aircraft battery? And the Vietnamese general Pham Van Dong took me aside and he said, I'm really touched you say that, but this is not the Spanish Civil War, where people from abroad can come and fight, and die. This is a war being fought between us and the most technologically advanced nation in the world. Having foreigners coming in to fight with us would require a great deal of effort keeping you people alive, which would be a distraction from the war. So please don't make this request of us.

Chapter 3

The Soviet Union
and Its Satellite States

Oliver Stone: We've talked about some of the cataclysmic events after World War II when the West expressed itself aggressively in changing governments. And we mustn't forget what happened in Greece in 1947. Could you talk about that?

Tariq Ali: Well, the Greek civil war was a very vicious, bloody war involving virtually every single family in Greece. Families were divided, families split up.

Like the Spanish Civil War?

Like the Spanish Civil War. The Greeks still call it "Churchill's War" because Churchill was so attached to the Greek right and to the Greek royal family that he did not want that country to be changed in any way after the war. The Russians had done the deal at Yalta, deciding that Greece was to be part of the Western sphere of influence. And Stalin was anything if not daft-minded when sticking to his deals. So he told the Greeks you have to behave yourselves. But a group of independent Greeks—they were communists, but more sympathetic to Tito and the Yugoslavs than to Stalin—led by a legendary leader, Aris Velouchiotis, said, we're going to continue on fighting. So, the war continued. The Russians couldn't do much about it, but Churchill did. And it was prosecuted with real viciousness and vigor until they defeated the communists.

That war still has echoes today. Recently I was in a part of Greece called Pelion, near Salonika. We were walking through a village, and a Greek friend said there was a big massacre in this village during the civil war, and this is the cemetery for all the communists who died. These events don't go away, you know. They stay. People remember them. Then something else happens, an eruption totally unrelated to that war, and all these things come up again. A police officer who ordered police to fire on student protesters, his father fought for the right in the civil war. History never goes away, which is why, when I'm speaking especially to younger people, I always say to them that history is present. You may not know it, but almost everything that happens is related to something in the past. You can't understand the present otherwise.

In Greece didn't Churchill nakedly hand over British military power to the Americans, saying you finish the job?

Exactly. Though to be technically accurate, the handover was conducted by his Labour Party successor, Clement Attlee, who was under left-wing pressure on this issue from his own party and was relieved to hand over the baby and the filthy bathwater to Truman. The same thing happened in Greece as happened in Saudi Arabia, as happened in other parts of the world where decaying empires handed over their functions to the United States. The United States took over the Greek civil war, and they regard that as a victory. They won that civil war. And many of the officers who carried out the coup d'état in Greece in 1967, imposing a military dictatorship, had fought in the civil war on the side of the West and had been friends ever since.

We've been talking about the Western reaction to World War II, and America's expansion as an empire afterward, displacing the British. Can we talk about the Soviet expansion of that era? Did Soviet aggressiveness provoke a Western response?

The Soviet leadership, Stalin and his successors, were tough on their own populations, but, by and large, they were very careful not to provoke the West. They kept to the deals they had made, both during and after the war. Churchill, Stalin, and Roosevelt had agreed at Yalta that Eastern Europe, with the countries named on a piece of paper, would be a part of the Soviet sphere of influence, and the Russians then took that seriously. Whether this piece of paper should have been signed at all is another question, but it was Then the Russians said, Eastern Europe is ours, we were attacked by the Germans through Poland, through Czechoslovakia, so we're going to control these countries now. That's been agreed to. And then they did something really foolish and shortsighted. The United States made big strategic mistakes, and so did the Russians. To impose the Soviet system on countries like Czechoslovakia, Poland, Romania, and Bulgaria was unnecessary and wrong. In Czechoslovakia, there actually was an election held in 1948, and the Czech Communist Party emerged as a very large political force in its own right, with the Social Democrats only marginally stronger. Now it should have been perfectly possible to maintain Soviet influence within a social democratic and communist coalition in Czechoslovakia. I think the Czech Social Democrats would have agreed to such an arrangement, but this wasn't the way Stalin operated. Instead, you had to have a one-party state with the central committee, with a politburo, with a general secretary. That model was imposed on Eastern Europe. It was imposed on East Germany, where you also had a strong social-democratic party, which could have continued. Forcible mergers took place. So, sooner or later, people in these countries said, we don't like this whole style of government, and you had rebellions. The first in East Berlin, the worker's uprising in East Berlin, soon after Stalin's death, crushed by Soviet tanks. Then you had the uprising in Hungary in 1956, crushed by Soviet tanks.

The revolt in East Berlin in 1953 was called the worker's uprising because it was mainly the working class that said we don't like this system and the way it's organized. We'd like to be in power, but we're not in power. And after the East Berlin worker's uprising was crushed, Bertolt Brecht wrote this wonderful ten-line letter in the form of a poem to the central committee of the East German Communist Party. The poem is called "The Solution." He said, dear comrades, it seems to me that the problem is the people:

Would it not be easier
In that case for the government
To dissolve the people
And elect another?

And that question of Brecht's can be applied to many situations. Both sides of the Cold War imposed governments they liked and deposed governments they didn't like.

So the East Berlin uprising was crushed. Then the Hungarian uprising of 1956 was crushed. Then came, of course, the Soviet invasion of Czechoslovakia in August 1968, when Czechs were experimenting with what they called "socialism with a human face." Big debates opened up on Czech television. For the first time you had a television network and a press that was freer than many outlets in the West. I'll never forget seeing Czech political prisoners on a special television program confronting the prison guards and the officials who had ordered their arrest. Why did you do it? The effect this had on popular consciousness was staggering. In Czech newspapers, you had endless debates. Does socialism have to be a gray one-party state? Don't we want socialist democracy, where people can say what they want, say what they feel? And these debates were then beginning to be smuggled in underground publications from Czechoslovakia, *samizdat,* into the Soviet Union itself. When print workers in the Ukraine published some of the Czech manifestos on socialism and democracy, the Russians panicked. They said, this disease must be stopped. It's like a cancer, it could kill us unless we deal with it, and they intervened. The Soviet entry into Prague in August 1968 was, I think, the death knell of the Soviet Union itself. Many people gave up hope. Alexander Solzhenitsyn, the great Soviet novelist, someone who is regarded as being very right wing, and nationalistic, was asked once, when did you give up hope that the Soviet system could be reformed? And he said on the twenty-first of August, 1968, when Leonid Brezhnev and his central committee decided to invade Czechoslovakia. For me, that was the end. And he was right. And it was the end not only for Solzhenitsyn, but for the whole system. The Soviet bureaucracy didn't realize it then, because they never think ahead, but what they did meant that the system was bound to implode sooner or later.

Of course, another development that panicked Stalin was the emergence of an independent-minded communist leader who wasn't prepared to do his bidding in Yugoslavia. Tito made Stalin fearful because his model was quite attractive, not just in the Balkans. The Greek communists were attracted by the Yugoslav model, as were many in Eastern Europe. They said, if Tito can be independent minded, why can't we? Why do we have to be under the Soviet thumb? And this encouraged the crushing of dissent within the communist parties and the communist movements. In the big show trials that took place in 1948 and 1949 in Hungary, Poland, and Czechoslovakia, the charge was not simply that you were an agent of Western imperialism. You were also labeled an "agent of Titoite revisionism." They didn't want to lose control, and that was very shortsighted of them.

We know there was a Russian Empire in the eighteenth and nineteenth centuries. We know they fought Poland and various countries, but when was the Soviet Empire at its height?

The tsarist empire had been an internal empire. Russia added countries on its borders, much like the United States did in its early days. And these countries were then pretty much assimilated, though not completely assimilated. And it was only in the early 1990s that they began to want to move away. And that, too, largely because that was a direction in which the West wanted to take them. But the Eastern European countries weren't an empire in the traditional sense, because it was largely a political empire, a socio-political empire, more than an economic one, and that's what made it very different from the West.

Was the Soviet Union able to extract raw minerals from their satellite countries? Or you're saying was it a trade policy that was highly favorable to the Soviet Union?

It was a trade policy, which was highly favorable to the Soviet Union in the sense that these countries were forced to buy Soviet goods or the economies were run in such a way that they were very heavily interdependent with the Soviet Union. But often the Soviet Union gave out more than it got back.

Such as in Cuba?

Cuba is a classic example of that. And even in East Germany, though they did dismantle a lot of factories in East Germany immediately after the war, so it took the East Germans a long time to recover, whereas what the United States was doing in West Germany was exactly the opposite, rebuilding the country in order to make it a showcase for the market. And they succeeded in doing that. The Russians didn't do that.

How do you respond to the argument that, at the end of the day, the countries under the influence of the American empire to a large degree have prospered, such as Japan, and to a certain degree, Latin America, and to a certain degree elites in Africa, and certainly Western Europe—whereas the Soviet empire made Hungary, Czechoslovakia, and Poland, which were rich countries at one point, poor?

Well, the argument against that is that Eastern European countries were, with the exception of Czechoslovakia, largely economically underdeveloped. Poland was a very undeveloped, largely peasant country. East Germany, of course, was part of the old Germany, but Allied bombing had destroyed Dresden, which was an East German city. The Soviet Union didn't have the wherewithal to rebuild these countries. It was mainly interested in rebuilding itself. We have to remember that the Russians suffered more during the Second World War than any other country in Europe. You know, they lost twenty million people. Their industries were destroyed, smashed. The United States lost people, but American cities were never bombed or attacked. What the United States did after the Second World War is unique in imperial history. They rebuilt their old rivals and brought them up to speed economically. No one has ever done that before, and I doubt whether any power will do it again. And the reason they did that is because they perceived that communism was a threat. They couldn't allow these countries to go under because they would become very susceptible to communism. They had to be built up.

The Russians provided countries with a crude but effective infrastructure, a social structure. Education was free, health was free, housing was heavily subsidized. It was a sort of public utility socialism. You didn't have freedom, but if you were a citizen in these countries, this is what you got. And you travel to these countries now, as I sometimes do, and the number of people who come up and say to you, we miss that period because that is all gone, is legion. So they did it in their own way. And the United States did it in its own way, creating rich elites in all these countries where the conditions of the poor didn't necessarily improve.

How about the middle class?

There was a large middle class in some of them. Not all the Latin American countries developed a large middle class, but some of them did, Brazil for instance. In the Soviet satellite states of Eastern Europe, you also saw the development of a middle class, but with constrictions and restrictions.

France certainly was very poor after the war, and it did come back.

But this is the point I'm making: all these countries came back because of the Marshall Plan. The aim of the Marshall Plan was to rebuild Western European capitalism and Japanese capitalism. Why? Because we were now in a battle to the death against the communists, who have a different social system. So we have to show them that our social and political system is much better, which is why, if you compare the media that existed in the 1950s through the 1970s in the United States, and in most of the European countries, there was far more diversity, discussion, debate on the networks, in the press than there is today. Many, many more divergent voices were allowed to write then now that they no longer have to demonstrate this to anyone. You can censor at will, you can marginalize voices you don't like. At that time they couldn't do this as much because they were trying to show our big rivals: this is how we're different than you. And it was effective. Lots of these German friends said we used to watch West German television, and see people like you on it, saying things that we could never say against our government, and that had an impact on us.

Could you talk about the conflicts over the division of East and West Berlin?

The Soviet Union's decision to impose a blockade on West Berlin in 1948 was meant to show the West that they were not totally cowed. All the pro-Soviet people had been chucked out of governments in most of Western Europe, France in particular. The Cold War had begun. And the Soviet Union thought, why don't we make a bid for West Berlin and make Berlin the capitol of our Germany. That will show the West that we can't be taken for granted, they can't just ride right over us. And they imposed a blockade. Whether they really thought that they would get their way is difficult to know—I'm sure it's in the archives somewhere—but certainly that blockade was broken. Another reason they wanted the blockade was because it was an anomaly to have Western armies in the middle of a country that had been partitioned. So there was a strategic element there. But certainly they went about it the wrong way, and they didn't have much support.

My father was an economist. He was actually on Eisenhower's economic staff at one point, and he worked in Berlin. He told me that the Soviets were trying to steal US currency printing plates. Apparently there was a lot of counterfeiting going on. There was disparate currencies, and the Soviets couldn't keep their population in check or content with a black market, such as it was.

This is absolutely true. The Soviets couldn't compete with the West economically. They certainly couldn't compete with the United States economy, which had emerged from the Second World War much more strengthened. And so they thought, let's end this anomaly of a Western showcase right on our doorstep.

Are you suggesting you don't fault the Soviets for building the Berlin Wall, then?

Well, I do fault them for the wall because I think it was foolish to imagine that you can keep people in or change people's minds by building a wall. It never works like that. We find that time and time again. If people are really determined to do something against the power that either occupies them or controls them, they find a way do it.

Chapter 4

Pax Americana?

Oliver Stone: Conservatives take credit for Reagan ending the Cold War. I think the counterargument would be that the Soviet system had exhausted itself economically and that Afghanistan in some way presaged its own problems for the Soviet Union, as Iraq presaged some problems for the United States. I see some similarities the path the United States has traveled and the one the Soviets traveled.

Tariq Ali: When one system, the Soviet system and all that it entailed, collapsed, in its wake there was a triumphalism in the West for years. We won, we smashed you, we beat you, now we're dominant. And all over the world, no alternative appeared to be emerging to this narrative. And I think a complacency set in among US leaders. They felt that we can now do whatever we want, get away with whatever we want. There is no one to challenge us. The system is unbeatable. And that is always a dangerous frame of mind for any imperial power—to believe that nothing can effect you, because the world isn't like that. So the first challenge, curiously enough, came from South America, and it came from a continent that had experimented in neoliberalism. After all, the Chicago boys didn't try out neoliberalism in Britain first. They tried it out in Chile under Pinochet, and later in Argentina. So you begin to see the emergence of social movements in a number of Latin American countries—Bolivia, Ecuador, Venezuela—that are fighting against attempts to deprive them of certain things they liked, like free water, transport subsidies, things which in the scale of the world appear very tiny but are very important for the everyday life of many people. And these social movements then produced reactions. In the case of Venezuela, three thousand people trying to protest against the IMF rules were killed in the streets by the military.

This is pre-Chávez?

Pre-Chávez, yes. That's what produced Chávez. Chávez didn't drop from the sky. He was produced from within the army, an army that used to massacre its own people. And Chávez and a whole group of junior officers met and said, this is not what we were created for. The only purpose of a military is to defend the country from outside invasion, and yet we've been used to kill our own people. That's how a dissenting group emerged inside the Venezuelan army.

Related developments were taking place in other parts of South America. In Bolivia, the neoliberal government decided to sell the water supply of Cochabamba to a subsidiary of Bechtel, the US corporation. And one of the things the water privatizers got the government to do was to pass a law saying that, from now on, it was illegal for poor people to go onto their roof and collect rainwater in receptacles because that challenged their monopoly of water. There's an uprising, an insurrection. The military intervened, a kid was shot to death, others were injured. More people came out, and they began to win. And these victories in South America were the first big sign that the old order could not be maintained, that things were changing. That the Washington consensus, postcommunist world ruled by the IMF, the World Bank, the WTO no longer could carry on that the same way in South America. Interestingly, these movements were also throwing up political leaders, and these political leaders were winning elections democratically. So you had a big shift away from the guerrilla warfare phase of South American politics, toward mass involvement in democracy, which everyone should have been cheering. I certainly was. Politicians are promising people certain things, and they're getting elected, and they're now trying to deliver on those promises. It was totally misunderstood in my opinion, deliberately so by the Bush administration, which tried to crush all these developments, organizing military coups, backing the most reactionary people in these countries.

Bush, Junior?

Bush, Junior. Bush, Junior did all that, backed by Cheney, and Condoleezza Rice in a very reactionary state department.

What about Clinton in Bosnia?

The intervention by the United States in Bosnia, seen by many people as humanitarian, turned out to be a straightforward attempt to increase American power and influence. So you have now a big permanent US missile base in Tuzla, and one of the largest helicopter bases ever in Kosovo. So this was the expansion of US power after the end of the Cold War, but the real resistance in terms of countries began in South America. And that is where it has remained ever since, with this exception: what's happened now is that the collapse of the neoliberal system, the bursting of the bubble, means the whole world now is waiting for alternatives.

I think it is quite possible that this particular world economic crisis, which is by no means over, is going to change people's ideas again. To what extent and in what direction we will see. But suddenly the South American experience becomes very important because these leaders who have been attacked in the media, the Bolivarians attacked as crazy, wild people, now seem very sober. And a new administration in Washington is having to deal with them rationally as elected politicians who represent their people. So if this example spreads to other continents, we could be in for interesting times again.

And everywhere we see taxpayers' money being used to bail out the rich. The whole ideology of neoliberalism is that the state is useless, the market will do everything. The market is supreme. The market collapses, and they fall on their knees before the state, and say to the state, "Help, please." And taxpayers' money goes to bail out every single bank in the Western world, more or less. But the effect this will have on popular consciousness, we are waiting to see.

So, we have seen these hugely important developments in South America. On the other hand, the economic center of the world has moved eastward. China is the new workshop of the world. Every cheap product you can buy all over the world is produced in China. And when the economy moves in such a big way, can politics be far behind? So the question that will haunt the twenty-first century is whether a new imperial power is emerging on a global scale to challenge the United States from the east. Will this happen? What will the United States do to block it? These are the questions now, which can only be understood by seeing the history of what has happened in the preceding two centuries. You can't run away from history. I don't think we will have a repeat of the First World War, because that would mean obliteration. On the other hand, the big question, which couldn't be asked a hundred years ago but has to be asked now, is put at its simplest, does the world have the resources for every single family to live like an American middle-class family lived in the 1950s and 1960s? And I think the answer is no. The world doesn't have the resources to do that. In which case, what is the point of this crazed, endless competition? Wouldn't it be better to find a different way of living for people all over the world?

You're talking about global problems, but you don't have much respect for one of the bodies that was allegedly established to address such problems, the United Nations, for instance. Is that correct?

Yes, this is true. I don't go for the international institutions. I think a lot can be done regionally. Here again, I return to the one example we have of a certain amount of regional cooperation in South America. I'm not one of those who thinks that what is going on in South America is a revolution, even though some of the leaders, such as Chávez, call it that. Essentially what is going on is that elected politicians are pushing through important social-democratic reforms to benefit the poor. That is very important in itself. One doesn't have to give it a new coloration. That's what they're doing. And the fact that, over the last fifty years, the Cubans have created a social infrastructure that produces more doctors per person in the population than any other country in the world, and these doctors can be provided as human capital in return for other things to Latin America and Africa is an amazing development. So when Hugo Chávez is confronted by a strike of middle-class professionals and the hospitals are closing down, he rings his friend Fidel Castro and within a few days, sixteen to twenty thousand Cuban doctors with their cheap medicines are on planes, coming over to set up clinics in the poorest parts of the country. That has an impact on people, including people who disagree with you.

I'm not saying that the world is going to be just changed like this everywhere, but for countries to collaborate regionally becomes important. Why shouldn't China, Japan, and the Korean Peninsula form a sort of a union, like the European Union? Why? Because the United States won't let it happen.

Why is that?

Because the United States sees the Far East as the biggest threat to its global hegemony. The Japanese, unlike the Germans, have not even been allowed a foreign policy of their own since the Second World War. They more or less do what they're told. This is dangerous, because it could give rise to dangerous forms of nationalism again, which wouldn't be good either for Japan or anyone else. What might be better is if the Japanese, the Chinese, the Koreans were encouraged to work together. Within that framework you could settle the North Korean question as well.

You realize there's a lot of antipathy between these three countries?

Of course, but there was a lot of antipathy between the Germans and the English, between the Germans and the French in Europe. Despite the bad history, there is nothing on earth now to stop these countries collaborating with each other,

Well, the Japanese were apparently so brutal in China and Korea that it's difficult for the Chinese to accept that the Japanese will not apologize for any of this.

Well, that is true, but I think an apology doesn't cost very much. The Germans are having to pay for what they did by reparations to Israel forever.

The Germans have apologized.

They have.

But the Japanese have not.

No, you're right. Has the United States apologized to them for using nuclear weapons?

No, nor to Vietnam.

No, nor to the Vietnamese. What I'm suggesting is not an easy way out. And there are lots of obstacles in its path, but that's the way things should go. I think we need to strengthen regional corporation for the world to pull out of the crisis and for something decent to happen.

You have written about Israel and Pakistan as confessional states. Pakistan is a division from India. Israel is a division from Palestine. Germany, Korea, and Vietnam were also created through separation. But these you would not say are confessional states, Korea, Germany, and Vietnam. So among the divisional states, the confessional states have turned out to be more dangerous. That's what you are saying?

I am, though in the case of Pakistan, the country broke up in 1971, when East Pakistan split off and became Bangladesh, which reduced its effectiveness as a state and severely damaged its ideology. The Israelis, by contrast, have been slowly accumulating more and more land, occupying more and more territory. But in both cases the elites are fairly hardened, implacable people who do what they think best, whether or not they have the support of their populations. The Israelis do have the support of their population. The Pakistanis don't. Nonetheless, in both these cases, it is not impossible to conceive that at the end of this century, Pakistan will be part of a larger union while preserving its state structures—a South Asian Union with India, Bangladesh, Sri Lanka, Nepal makes a lot of sense—and that, at some stage, the Israeli population will realize that enough is enough, and that the Palestinians will realize they are never going to get an independent state of any significance, and there will be a move toward a single-state solution of Palestine and Israel in which Jews, Muslims, Christians, smaller minorities, will be able to live together. I don't think there is another way out.

You quote Thomas Friedman, the *New York Times* columnist, as saying it's not just McDonald's but McDonnell Douglas that you need to run the empire.

Yes.

And what did he mean by that?

He meant that essentially it is US military power that is decisive in this world, and that helps to maintain McDonald's all over the world. You know, there are now US military bases or installations in sixty or seventy countries of the world. That is a very heavy presence for the United States. And it doesn't help them particularly, whether in Afghanistan or Iraq, to have these extensions. This projection of US power not only produces anger and resentment, it has a destabilizing effect. The Russians, for instance, in Georgia, are saying, if you can intervene militarily in Kosovo, we can do it in Georgia. Who are you to tell us what to do? The Indians are saying, if terrorists from a country hate you, you occupy that country. How can you tell us not to do the same thing? So this pattern of American behavior has not created a world that is moving toward peace and stability, which they claimed was their aim.

A sort of *Pax Americana*? There would be one power, and it would be benevolent?

Yes.

It doesn't work that way.

It doesn't work that way. Even the Roman Empire, which had the *Pax Romana*, couldn't maintain its dominion for too long, and began to crack up. The United States on its own terms is already a very, very large country with a huge population and enormous resources. The best example it could set in the world is to put its own house in order. I mean, the fact is, the United States doesn't have a health service. The education system leaves a lot to be desired. When New Orleans was flooded in the wake of Hurricane Katrina, and all of those people were left unprotected, large numbers of my American friends in New York and the West Coast said they had no idea things were so bad. And that worried me. Why didn't you?

I remember during the last election, people were energized the world over when they saw huge numbers of kids turning up for Obama's election campaign. People said this couldn't happen in Europe, because in Europe the bulk of kids between eighteen and twenty-six tend not to vote these days. So we are seeing a process where, because of the economic system and the way it offers no possibility of any alternatives, democracy itself is becoming hollowed out as a process. And people are saying if the choice we were offered between center left and center right in Europe, or between the Congress Party and the BJP in India, or between party X and party Y in some other country is really not very deep, then what the hell is the point of voting? And, again here, the example which contradicts all that is Latin America where you have people who are offered choices, different choices, and who go and vote according to their beliefs. Some wanted to stay with the old, some wanted the new. So which of these trends is going to win out remains to be seen. I think a lot will depend on how the economy develops.

Let's talk about the economy for a moment. What is Marxism, first of all?

Marxism is essentially a form of understanding history. I think Marx's most important contribution theoretically was to say that history is essentially, though not exclusively, a struggle between contending classes, from the days of antiquity to now. And that assumption, which seems now relatively straightforward, transformed the way we look at the world and how we study history.

The second thing Marx did was to explain the ways in which capitalism functions. The drive to profit, which is the dominant drive in capital, determines everything. And then there are some incredibly prescient passages in which he talks about fictive capital, fictional capital, the system using money that it doesn't have and imploding. And he points out that this cycle will repeat itself in the history of capitalism as long as the system lasts. He never describes in detail what an alternative to the capitalist system would look like. That is not his function. That is left to other people who make revolutions to describe. But he says that the gravediggers of the system are produced by the system itself, the system will let people down, that they will rise and topple it.

So for Marx, the countries most suited for socialism are the countries where the productive forces and technology have developed the most. According to this conception, the United States would be the country most suited for a rapid transition from one system to the other because all it needs is a planned system. Whereas most of the revolutions, if not all the revolutions that took place, happened in countries that were very backward—tsarist Russia, China. Cuba was pretty backward, too, in many ways.

You have written that we only had one shot at socialism, and it failed. But there have been many shots at capitalism.

This is true. I say this because capitalism has failed numerous times. I don't know whether there's agreement, but, from 1825, there have been dozens and dozens of capitalist cycles of boom and bust, boom, bust, collapse. I mean, certainly we can remember the big ones, but there have been minor ones as well. Yet that system is always permitted to revive, or is revived, as we are seeing today. And the socialists, the communists and the socialists, had one attempt, which lasted seventy-five years and then collapsed, and everyone says it's over. And in my opinion, that particular style of communism and that particular attempt may be over, but there is absolutely no reason why people shouldn't think of better systems than the existing one, without going back to the worst of what the Soviet system was.

The United States, ironically, is in a position where the state has a large ownership in the economy now.

This is true, but how is it using this stake? Is it for state capitalism or is it to create a public utility capitalism, which is certainly possible now by injecting a lot of state money into public utilities that would produce for need and not for profit. I mean, that is I think what should be done, and what a rational capitalist state would now do. What I would say to these guys at the banks and mortgage companies and investment houses is you failed. We gave you a big chance, we backed you up. It's not that the state didn't intervene. The state provided the basis for you guys to get away with murder, to make billions, and you let us down very badly, you failed us, so now we are not going to let you do it for the next fifty years. We're going to build and develop public utilities, which we are doing to control, run, and pay for. And this is going to benefit our population far more than anything you ever did. I mean, there are some things that people deserve by right, including health, education, some form of affordable dwelling—which in Europe social democracy used to promise to try and deliver, and often did deliver.

In smaller countries.

In smaller countries.

It's harder to do in the Soviet Union, the United States, or China, I would imagine.

It is true though, to be fair, I do not think the Chinese breakthrough, because that's what we have to call it, would have been possible had they not had a revolution and created a very high-level class of graduates, scientists, and technicians. And I think that explains why they're economically way ahead of India. The raising and lifting of the culture of the country, producing these people who came from very humble backgrounds, is actually the basis of the current transformation of China.

Would you describe yourself as a pessimist of the intellect and an optimist of the will?

I would. We are now for instance coming to a time when the car as the big icon of capitalism, as the only way for nations to move forward, is facing collapse. This is not just the rising price of oil, but also because the demand for American cars is falling. Why can't a rational government in the United States develop an effective public transport system, including rebuilding trains, rebuilding tracks? It's the one thing the Europeans are beginning to do now.

Or pass a tax on carbon emissions?

Yes. Pass a tax. It's a simple political decision. It's a matter of willpower. Instead we see the same paralysis that existed at the end of the Roman Empire, when the population could not be imposed on for anything; they had to be provided with spectacle, as Octavio Paz said. Now we have the spectacle of television. And reality television, in which everyone is encouraged to be a celebrity.

Yes.

I mean, it's quite astonishing the way this has happened.

Has it hit Pakistan yet?

It's not hit Pakistan, but then you sometimes feel that the whole of Pakistan is like a reality television show anyway.

But it's hit India.

It has hit India in a big way, with disastrous effects on the Indian media. I mean, the Indian newspapers used to be among the best in the world. If you look at them now, they're filled with trivia and trash. Pakistan's television stations and newspapers and magazines are at the moment infinitely superior to India's. They have not gone down that route. So you can see and hear debates on the independently owned private television networks and in Pakistani newspapers, that you don't at all in India. It's quite a worrying development.

You've written that the fate of the Jews, events in Palestine and Congo, are the responsibility of "bourgeois civilization." I suppose that's a Marxist term, right?

Right.

You blame bourgeois civilization?

Well, what I say is that, whatever way you want to describe it, it was European capitalist civilization that was responsible ultimately for the death of six million Jews, yes.

And the Congo?

And the Congo.

And World War I? There are a lot of people who died in World War II.

Yes, absolutely.

You think it's the result of bourgeois civilization?

I think there is no other way to explain it. That and competitiveness between different strands of this civilization.

So the competition that I went through in boarding school, which was so cruel and is not the way out—we are told it makes you a better man, a stronger man, but at the same time—

—it's very destructive. Yes, it's also very destructive. With individuals, it can have certain negative effects on the psyche of the individual. But when states engage in competition, it leads to the loss of millions of lives.

But our state is created by people from Eden, Harrow, Choate, St. Paul's, Andover, Exeter, Yale, Harvard. These are the people whom you call the state intellectuals.

These are people who run the state. This is absolutely true. In the case of the British Empire, the system of private schooling expanded phenomenally, and some schools were created explicitly to train imperial administrators. And this happens in the United States, too. Many, many people from the elite universities, Ivy League universities, used to go, and still go, into the foreign service, run the state department, and so on. The system and its administrators reproduce themselves through this elite educational system. But the question is: are they going to repeat past histories and fight each other to a standstill and, in the process, destroy the planet? That's the big question now.

Chapter 5

Blowback

Oliver Stone: Could you talk about the concept of "blowback"?

Tariq Ali: A very honest, decent, strong-minded, truthful American scholar, Chalmers Johnson, who had worked as a consultant for the Central Intelligence Agency in the 1950s and came from an old naval family, wrote a book in 2000 called *Blowback*. The book offers a strong critique of US foreign policy. His basic argument was that, given what we have been doing to the rest of the world, it's only a matter of time before some people take the law into their own hands and decide to hit us. And he developed this argument with great skill. When the book came out, it was either attacked by critics or ignored. He was astonished at the viciousness with which the book was received. I wasn't, actually. But immediately after 9/11, the book, which had been ignored until then, took off by word of mouth. The book sold and sold and sold, and Chalmers became a world figure. It was translated everywhere.

The idea of "blowback" was about the American support of Arabic Jihadists in Afghanistan, who were fighting the Soviets.

Yes, and many people warned the United States that they were playing with fire, but as Zbigniew Brzezinski said, it's a small price to pay for bringing down the Soviet Empire. No, the exact words he used were even cruder. He said what are a few "stirred-up Muslims" compared to bringing down the Soviet Empire? Well, we know how that story ends.

The "war on terror."

I always found the "war on terror" an odd concept. The history of terrorism is real, it exists, and what it means usually is small groups of people, sometimes in the hundreds, sometimes a few thousand, who decide that the way to change the world is to hit strategic targets. The anarchists in the late nineteenth and early twentieth centuries used to try to kill presidents, heads of state, the tsar of Russia. Sometimes they succeeded, but usually they failed. In Paris, they would bomb bourgeois cafés, and say "we're killing the bourgeoisie." This sort of nonsense has happened for a long time. It never really changes anything, but it makes people who carry out these acts feel good. It was referred to as "propaganda of the deed." We're showing we hate X and Y by doing this, even though none of these people they were attacking crumbled as a result. Then you had a big wave of these politics in the 1960s. You had the Weather Underground in this country. They targeted installations, and sometimes they killed themselves by accident. And during this period you also had terrorist groups in Italy, Germany, Japan. Then you had right-wing groups in the United States. I mean, the Oklahoma bombings were carried out by a guy who went hunting with the Aryan Nation, a white supremacist group. You had Cuban terrorists trying to destabilize the Cuban regime, backed in this case by the United States. The foundation of Israel is linked to terrorist groups, in particular the Irgun, which destroyed the King David Hotel. One of the members of the Irgun was Menachem Begin, later given the Nobel Peace Prize with Anwar Sadat of Egypt. When Golda Meir, the former Israeli prime minister, was asked for her comments, she said, I don't know whether they deserved the Nobel Prize, but they certainly deserve an Oscar for acting.

The history of the world is littered with examples of terrorism. So why make this act of terror so different? The spectacle and scale of it doesn't make the people who did it different from other terrorists. And we now know from the various books that have come out that immediately after 9/11, senior members of the Bush regime said, we must now use this attack to get our way. Everyone knows that their basic gut instinct was to attack Iraq, not Afghanistan. They wanted to punish Saddam Hussein for something he hadn't done. So the war on terror essentially became a holdall for US foreign policy getting its own way wherever it wanted to, locking up people, and picking up people all over the world with the help of its allies in the name of this war on terror.

But why Iraq, of all the places on earth?

For two reasons. Some people within the Bush administration felt that Iraq was unfinished business since 1991. That, at the end of the Gulf War the United States should have toppled Saddam Hussein, but Bush, Senior's advisers had said don't do it—and, as we now know, for good reason. Bush, Junior. and his advisers wanted to complete what that administration hadn't done, and what Clinton hadn't done, even though Clinton had gone a long way in punishing Iraq, with his US ambassador to the United Nations, Madeleine Albright, defending the deaths of five hundred thousand children as a result of these sanctions.

How many children died?

Lesley Stahl of *60 Minutes* asked Madeleine Albright, is the death of more than half a million children as a result of these sanctions justified? And Albright replied, yes, "we think the price is worth it." Now when you have leaders with this mentality trying to teach lessons on morality to the rest of the world, it doesn't quite wash.

You said there were other reasons for picking Iraq.

Another reason for targeting Iraq after 9/11 was that the Israelis didn't like the existence of Iraq as an independent state, with an independent army. Even though Iraq didn't have nuclear weapons, the Israelis felt it was always possible that this army would be used against them in the future, failing to see that the reason for Arab hostility to Israel is linked to their failure to do what they should have done regarding the Palestinians. So there was a lot of pressure from the Israelis as well, and I think that pressure played a much more important part than it should have in impelling the Bush administration to take Iraq.

The Pentagon would also have known that as they knew that the Iraqi army was quite diminished, that Iraq barely had any armaments left to wage a real struggle, that the Iraqi air force had been destroyed. Iraq was already a defeated country, defeated by sanctions, wrecked by the years of US bombings in the "no-fly zones" in the northern parts of the country.

So we were looking for a weakling?

A weakling to demonstrate American power. And, you know, a number of US spokesmen, in their arrogance at the time, said, we did it because we could.

Could you talk about the doctrine of preemptive war?

The doctrine of preemptive war is totally against the UN Charter. The UN Charter was meant to guard nations against so-called preemptive wars. The only condition for waging a war is if there is real evidence that you're about to be attacked. And the reason that was written into the UN Charter is because the biggest defender of preemptive wars was Adolph Hitler. Every time he invaded a nation, whether it was Poland, Czechoslovakia, or Austria, he would say, our interests are under threat. Or in the case of Czechoslovakia, the minority German population in the Sudetenland is under threat from the majority Czechs. Or in Poland, they threatened our security. We want Danzig back. Why should we have a Polish corridor? All these things were perfected, which is why the UN Charter was written to prevent that. And Wolfowitz, Cheney,—

And Perle—

—Perle, all these guys, with the journalists supporting them, and egging them on. Christopher Hitchens, Kanan Makiya, and the House Arabs, as I've referred to them. Trained to bark loyally when the United States goes to war, "you will be welcomed, you will be greeted with sweets and flowers, yes, come and liberate, liberate us, liberate us." All these people were braying away. And so, Bush made the jump, and the result is what we see. More than a million Iraqis have died since the occupation of that country by the United States. It's no good saying, "But we haven't killed all of them," as some are prone to do. You may not have killed all of them, but you created the conditions in which they could be killed by occupying that country.

And Afghanistan now?

Afghanistan now is a total and complete mess. Everyone knows it. President Obama knows it. His advisers know it.

Is the United States in another Vietnam-style quagmire in Afghanistan?

I think the only way it could become a Vietnam is if they sent in at least a quarter of a million more troops. I think then they would be in a quagmire. There would be heavy US casualities. They would kill a lot of people. They would wreck that country. The war would spill over into Pakistan, involve large segments of the Pakistani population and military on both sides, and there would be hell to pay. Afghanistan is a mess because the government the United States put in is a totally corrupt government, which is feathering its own nest, stealing massive amounts of money from the foreign aid coming in, not doing anything for the people.

Then, on top of corruption, there are too many civilian casualities, too many deaths. You become dependant on air power, as in Vietnam. And the drones come and bomb villages, they bomb innocents, and that is creating a situation that is unwinnable. The British couldn't defeat the Afghanis, the Russians couldn't, and the United States is not going to defeat them either, unless they wipe out half the population and occupy that country permanently with half a million US troops, which I think won't wash. The region wouldn't bear it, and the US population would have something to say.

You know, it's a mystery to me why Obama didn't use his election victory to say we're going to end that mess. We've got to pull out. Some of his advisers know that situation better than anyone else. So an exit strategy to get the United States and NATO out of Afghanistan is needed before the situation gets only worse.

What about women's rights in Afghanistan?

It was shameful when Cherie Blair and Laura Bush went on television to justify the Afghan intervention by saying it's a war to liberate women. I pointed out at the time that, if this was the case, it would be the first time in history that an imperial power had waged war to liberate women. It wasn't going to happen, and it didn't happen. The condition of women is as bad as ever, and these are reports from women's groups in Afghanistan.

So what would you do?

I don't think anything can be done from the outside. I think in order to change these conditions, change has to come from the inside. There was a very interesting development when pro-Taliban groups in Pakistan publicly flogged a poor woman. Pakistani television showed a video of the flogging, and there were protests in large cities in Pakistan. Women's groups denounced it. The chief justice summoned the attorney general to a court and said our laws are being violated, what on earth are you doing about this? Then the Taliban retreated, and said it wasn't us, we didn't do it. So people in Pakistan are now saying, no, these are not "outside values." It was never the case that we liked anyone being flogged. Public floggings and all that is something that started in Pakistan during the Zia-ul-Haq military dictatorship. We never had it before, and you're now doing it to women. That's not part of our law, either.

And Sharia law?

This is a Wahabi version of Sharia law, which is not accepted by many Shias or an overwhelming majority of Sunni legal scholars. It is a sectarian Wahabi interpretation. And why has this now suddenly landed in Pakistan? Why should women suffer? I mean, you know, women under control of these wretched Wahabists suffer more than Muslim women did in the medieval period in Islam. And that is something they don't even realize. And honor killings, which are going on in different parts of the world. I mean, I know that it's not exclusively Islam. We had honor killings in South America, But the point I'm trying to make is that in a world without any positive values, in a world totally obsessed with money and celebrity culture and all this, people are becoming slightly crazy.

Do you think that's new?

It's not new, but in the 1940s and 1950s, the 1960s and 1970s, people did think the world could be changed for the better. And when that feeling goes away, then all these retrogressive groups and movements come to the fore.

Could you talk about the use of torture in Guantánamo, elsewhere?

Well, the fact that torture has become acceptable again is all part of the war on terror logic. It's right to torture because we have to torture them to get information from them, they're going to attack us. This is an old, old argument which goes back to the medieval era, to the Inquisition. That's where we are now. And if you can't torture them in the United States proper, torture them in Guantánamo. If you can't torture them in Guantánamo, torture them at the Bagram base and prison in Afghanistan, where the Russians used to torture people. The United States and its allies are torturing people in exactly the same place. And there are horrific stories coming out of there. Or use the Pakistani torture system, or the Egyptian, or the Syrian. Send in our people to soften up a guy until he tells the truth, never asking how do you know it's the truth? This guy was waterboarded, god knows how many times, Khalid Sheikh Mohammed. I mean, what value does his testimony have in any court of law after that? You're basically destroying anything you might have got from a serious interrogation of these people. So these are the values. You know, after the 9/11 attacks, Bush and Blair used to say, we will never let these people change our way of life. But you have.

Chapter 6

The Revenge of History

Oliver Stone: You write in *The Clash of Fundamentalisms*, "There is a universal truth that pundit and politician need to acknowledge: slaves and peasants do not always obey their masters. Time and time again, in the upheavals that have marked the world since the days of the Roman Empire, a given combination of events has yielded a totally unexpected eruption. Why should it be any different in the twenty-first century?"

Tariq Ali: It won't be any different, of that I am pretty sure. We can't predict what these events will be or where they will happen, but they will surprise the world. It's precisely because one knows what has happened in history before that one maintains a certain degree of optimism. The Latin American developments were not foreseen by anyone. No one expected that Venezuela, a country that was barely known in the world, would suddenly become part of the "axis of hope," as I call it. Chávez put Venezuela on the world map. You know, the first time Chávez went to the Middle East, Al Jazeera interviewed him for one hour. Because Arab viewers hate subtitles, a very good actor read all his lines in Arabic. Chávez is anyway quite magnetic, but afterwards, the Al Jazeera producer who did this said to me, we had thousands and thousands of emails, more than we'd ever had. And 90 percent of these emails said, in one form or the other, when will the Arab world produce a Chávez?

Where could the next Chávez come from?

Well, it is difficult to predict exactly, but I think that South Asia and the Far East might throw some surprises at us, which we're not ready for. We talk about China as an economic giant but we very rarely talk about what the effects of this system are in China. Peasant uprisings, working-class factory occupations, a restless, turbulent intelligentsia, all these things could happen.

And is there a potential wild card in an internal economic collapse of the empire? Some people have suggested we cannot afford all these troops, all these bases.

Well, I think a lot will depend on the economy. A lot will depend on what the American public will do if the economy continues to go down like this. If the American population comes out and rebels against all this, well, that's the end for the empire. It can't continue.

It's very hard for the population to rebel against the military. That is always difficult historically.

Yes, but people might vote for someone who says, we've done too much abroad for too long, and the costs have been great for us, and now let's use that same energy to transform the shape of our country at home. If a politician were to say that at the present time, I think such a person would get a lot of support. Obama had possibilities, but it's obvious he's not going to go down that route. He might if there was a big popular movement in the United States demanding that. There isn't. But I think that is what is needed.

Another potential wild card that I would suggest is in the offing would be some large environmental crisis. That would shake everybody up fast.

Well, without any doubt. I mean, once that becomes obvious to most people. But, again, how do you then reorganize the world?

At that point it becomes necessary—

—essentially to work together, to plan, to have a planned economy.

There would be a plan right away?

There would be.

Would people be pulling out their Marxist textbooks on how to do it? Are there specifics?

Well, I don't think there are any good textbooks to show how good planning can work, but at least we now know how not to do it. And we know that the plan needs to involve the population as a whole, which needs to offer some oversight from below.

What is the best planned state in the world? Is it Switzerland?

I think it probably is one of the smaller Scandinavian ones. The Norwegians are quite well planned. The Cubans are well planned in terms of their social infrastructure. They've done it, and they've shown how it could be done.

But this would be perhaps the biggest surprise of all because people do keep saying, yes, it's going to happen, but they don't expect it to happen tomorrow.

No, and because so many people like living in the present—and are encouraged to live in the present—they don't want to think about tomorrow. They live for today.

You write that it's as if history has become subversive. The past has too much knowledge embedded in it, and therefore it's best to forget it and start anew. But as everyone is discovering, you can't do this to history. It refuses to go away. If you try to suppress it, it reemerges in a horrific fashion.

Precisely.

Do the particular origins of the US Empire make it in any way different, more prone to ignore or deny history?

When I think about the origins of the American Empire, the first thing that comes to mind, of course, is that the colonists began by destroying the native population they encountered, and this was linked to a religious fundamentalist belief in their own goodness and greatness. I mean, the fundamentalists who came here, the pilgrim fathers, had a way of thinking that wasn't basically different from that of the Wahabis or Osama bin Laden. In fact, there are lots of similarities between Protestant fundamentalism and Wahabi fundamentalism, and you see that in how they treat women, all the campaigns.

The Salem Witch Trials?

Exactly. You know, women are possessed by the devil. Beat it out of them. So that was the origin. Then you have slavery, the basis for much of the wealth generated inside the United States. Then you have the violent expansion of the empire, which is something Cormac McCarthy describes very well in one of his finest novels, *Blood Meridian*. Then you have the Civil War, which we are told is about the liberation of slaves, and which is partially to do with that, but which is essentially an attempt to unify the United States by force. So all this created the modern United States as we know it. And from the First World War onward the United States grew in size and influence, and became a dominant power, which after the Cold War has become an ultra-imperialism, unchallenged, unchallengeable militarily, very strong, without rivals. This is the first time in human history that an empire has been without any rivals. The Romans sometimes used to think that they were, but that's because they weren't totally aware of the strength of the Persians or even the Chinese. They thought in terms of the Mediterranean world, not globally. So, this is the first time that this has happened. And it made the leaders of this empire extremely complacent, who took the consent of their people for granted.

But what happens if this consent is suddenly withdrawn? Now the big problems confronting the empire at the moment are economic, the state of the economy at home, and military overstretch. Iraq is a disastrous war. Afghanistan is turning out to be the same thing. The empire's "backyard," as it has traditionally been known since the time of the Monroe Doctrine, is totally out of control, with a wave of radical politicians, the Bolivarian politicians, led by Hugo Chávez, backed by Evo Morales, and Rafael Correa, and the Cubans, and Bishop Lugo of Paraguay, and backed less strongly but also with the support of Lula in Brazil and Bachelet in Chile and Kirchner in Argentina, saying to the United States, we're not going to let you isolate us any longer. We're going to collaborate with each other. We won't let you use a single country to destroy another, as we've done in the past. And the leaders of the United States are now being compelled to look at this new face of Latin America.

Now it's a long way to go from here to say that this is going to break up the United States. I think people who talk about the automatic breakup of empires are wrong. It doesn't happen automatically. But the economic crisis, if it carries on like this, if the billions given to save the banks fail, then I think you could have unpleasant surprises in store for the rulers. They may not be surprises that people on the left particularly like, but they will be surprises. There will be a new mood, which asks, why are we spending so much abroad? Why should we bolster up these regimes and countries? What has it got to do with us? Let's improve our own country. And how such a movement develops remains to be seen. But I think one thing we have to say is that the triumphalism and euphoria that existed after the collapse of the Soviet Union has virtually gone. Everyone knows that it's a more difficult world that they have to confront.

It's not "the end of history"?

Far from the end of history, and far from simply being "the clash of civilizations." I mean, I think even Francis Fukuyama has acknowledged that the world has changed beyond what he'd imagined, and Samuel Huntington, in his last public work, moved beyond the clash of civilizations to warning of a clash within Christianity, saying that the white Anglo-Saxon Protestant elite in the United States faced a real challenge from the Hispanics, who he said are threatening our way of life. These are sort of Catholic Christians from South America who are threatening our way of life. He was wrong in that sense, but he was indirectly right in that the size of the Hispanic population in the United States is now larger than it's ever been. Their growth rates as a population in terms of demography are much, much higher than that of the non-Catholic sections of the population. And the new migrants from South America act as a bridge with South America. They're concerned about what happens in Chiapas in Mexico. They're concerned about Central America. They're concerned about the Bolivarians, concerned in a good way in many cases. And the young generation of Cubans in Florida don't want the United States to attack Cuba. So things are not the same as when Florida and other places were just nests of reaction, with old counterrevolutionaries coming to find a nice home. It's moved a lot beyond that. The interesting question, which in my more utopian moods I sometimes ponder, is whether the changes in South America might travel across this bridge via the Hispanic populations in the United States to produce something that none of us can foresee. Certainly the hegemony of the English language is being challenged in many American towns in the south.

I'd love for you to talk about Rudyard Kipling, who lost his son in World War I.

Kipling forced his young son to go and fight in the First World War. The boy couldn't see properly. He couldn't have passed any military board. But Kipling used his influence with the British government of the day, and the generals who knew him well, and said, my son is desperate to fight, you must take him into the army. So the boy went to fight in World War I, died fairly early on. And Kipling never really got over that. He wrote one poem in which said he said,

If any question why we died,
Tell them, because our fathers lied
And in "A Dead Statesman," he wrote,
I could not dig: I dared not rob:
Therefore I lied to please the mob.
Now all my lies are proved untrue,
And I must face the men I slew.
What tale should serve me here among
Mine angry and defrauded young?

And these beautiful lines are so applicable to Iraq, to Afghanistan, and to numerous other wars that are being fought in the twenty-first century, a hundred years after Kipling wrote those lines.

In your writings, you also cite Joseph Conrad, a Pole living in London.

Joseph Conrad was a great Polish writer who moved to London, learned English as a second language, and became one of its finest practitioners. He was very hostile to Belgian colonialism, and many European ones, but was very soft on the British because they had given him refuge. In his famous novel, *Heart of Darkness,* which is a description of King Leopold's horrors in the Congo, he wrote:

They were conquerors, and for that you want only brute force—
nothing to boast of, when you have it, since your strength is just
an accident arising from the weakness of others. They grabbed
what they could get for the sake of what was to be got. It was
just robbery with violence, aggravated murder on a great scale,
and men going at it blind—as is very proper for those who tackle
a darkness. The conquest of the earth, which mostly means the
taking it away from those who have a different complexion or
slightly flatter noses than ourselves, is not a pretty thing when
you look into it too much. What redeems it is the idea only.

And when you think about this, it really does apply to what
has been going on in the late twentieth and early twenty-first
centuries. And what Conrad and Kipling demonstrate is the con-
tinuities of history. You know, this is nothing new. It has been
going on. And the more people that know that these mistakes
were made by previous rulers, the better. They should be learned
from—and not repeated. If politicians are only destined to repeat
themselves historically, the world has a very sad fate ahead for it.

You quote an Iraqi poem, "On the Bird."

The history of poetry in Iraq is very interesting. The major poets
of Iraq happen to be communists. Most of them were exiled by
Saddam Hussein when he first came to power. And then soon, just
before the first Iraq war, Saddam Hussein realized that the population was missing them, and he sent a message to all three of
them, who were in different exiles, and said, why don't you come
and give one big poetry reading in Baghdad? There will be a mil-

lion people to listen to you. The Iraqi ambassador went to London and said this to Saadi Youssef, the greatest amongst them. And Saadi Youssef asked, who will guarantee our lives? When the ambassador took the message back to Iraq, Saddam Hussein said, tell them the blood on my neck will guarantee their lives. But they said that's not good enough, and didn't go. One of them, Mudhafar al-Nawab, who lived in exile in Damascus, wrote this poem:

I have accepted my fate
Is like that of a bird,
And I have endured all
Except humiliation.
Or having my heart
Caged in the Sultan's palace.
But dear God
Even birds have homes to return to.
I fly across this homeland
From sea to sea,
And to prison after prison, after prison,
Each jailer embracing the other.

A powerful poem.

Yes.

And on that note, thank you so much, Tariq.

It's been my great pleasure, Oliver.

James Porto

Oliver Stone has directed: *Wall Street: Money Never Sleeps* ('10), *W.* ('08), *World Trade Center* ('06), *Alexander* ('04), *Any Given Sunday* ('99), *U-Turn* ('97), *Nixon* ('95), *Natural Born Killers* ('94), *Heaven and Earth* ('93), *JFK* ('91), *The Doors* ('91), *Born on the Fourth of July* ('89), *Talk Radio* ('88), *Wall Street* ('87), *Platoon* ('86), *Salvador* ('86), *The Hand* ('81), and *Seizure* ('73). He's written or cowritten all of the above, with the exception of *U-Turn*, *World Trade Center*, *W.*, and *Wall Street: MNS*.

He's also written or cowritten: *Midnight Express* ('78), *Scarface* ('83), *Conan the Barbarian* ('82), *Year of the Dragon* ('85), *Evita* ('96), and *8 Million Ways to Die* ('86).

He's directed five documentaries: *Looking for Fidel* ('04), *Co-*

mandante ('03), *Persona Non Grata* ('03), *South of the Border* ('09), and *The Untold History of the United States* series for Showtime ('11). He's produced or coproduced: *The People vs. Larry Flynt* ('96), *The Joy Luck Club* ('93), *Reversal of Fortune* ('90), *Savior* ('98), *Freeway* ('96), *South Central* ('98), *Zebrahead* ('92), *Blue Steel* ('90), and the ABC mini-series *Wild Palms* ('93). An Emmy was given to him and his coproducer for the HBO film *Indictment: The Mc-Martin Trial*, and he was nominated for the documentary *The Last Days of Kennedy and King.*

Stone has won Oscars for directing *Born on the Fourth of July* and *Platoon*, and for writing *Midnight Express*. He was nominated for director (*JFK*) and cowriter (*Nixon*). He's also received three Golden Globes for directing (*Platoon, Born on the Fourth of July*, and *JFK*) and one for writing (*Midnight Express*).

Stone wrote a novel, published in 1997 by St. Martin's Press, entitled *A Child's Night Dream*, based on Stone's experiences as a young man. He is a contributor of some two hundred pages worth of essays on movies, culture, politics, and history to the book *Oliver Stone's USA*, edited by Robert Brent Toplin and published by the University Press of Kansas (2000). Stone wrote the afterword for a book of scholarly essays analyzing his film *Alexander* called "Oliver Stone's *Alexander*: Film, History, and Cultural Studies" (2009).

Stone was born September 15, 1946, in New York, New York. Prior to his film career, Stone worked as a schoolteacher in Vietnam, a taxi driver, messenger, production assistant, and sales representative. He served in the US Army Infantry in Vietnam in 1967–68. He was wounded twice and decorated with the Bronze Star for Valor. After returning from Vietnam, he completed his undergraduate studies at New York University Film School in 1971.

Nina Subin

Tariq Ali is a writer and filmmaker. He has written more than two dozen books on world history and politics, and seven novels (translated into over a dozen languages) as well as scripts for the stage and screen. He is an editor of *New Left Review* and lives in London. His website is http://tariqali.org.